DEALING WITH FINANCIAL RISK

OTHER ECONOMIST BOOKS

Emerging Markets
Guide to Analysing Companies
Guide to Business Modelling
Guide to Business Planning
Guide to Economic Indicators
Guide to the European Union
Guide to Financial Markets
Guide to Management Ideas
Numbers Guide
Style Guide

Dictionary of Business
Dictionary of Economics
International Dictionary of Finance

Brands and Branding
Business Ethics
Business Strategy
China's Stockmarket
E-trends
Globalisation
Successful Innovation
Successful Mergers
Wall Street

Essential Director
Essential Economics
Essential Finance
Essential Internet
Essential Investment
Essential Negotiation

Pocket Asia
Pocket Europe in Figures
Pocket World in Figures

DEALING WITH FINANCIAL RISK

David Shirreff

THE ECONOMIST IN ASSOCIATION WITH
PROFILE BOOKS LTD

Published by Profile Books Ltd
3A Exmouth House, Pine Street, London EC1R 0JH
www.profilebooks.com

Typeset in EcoType by MacGuru Ltd
info@macguru.org.uk

Printed in Great Britain by
Clays, Bungay, Suffolk

A CIP catalogue record for this book is available
from the British Library

ISBN 978 1 86197 591 1

The paper this book is printed on is certified by the © 1996 Forest Stewardship Council A.C. (FSC). It is ancient-forest friendly. The printer holds FSC chain of custody SGS-COC-2061

To Henry and George

Contents

Acknowledgements

I would like to thank Euromoney Institutional Investor for allowing me to draw liberally on articles that I wrote for *Euromoney* magazine in the 1990s, and IFCI Risk Institute on whose website my analysis of the Long-Term Capital Management crisis first appeared. For many thoughtful conversations on financial risk I would also like to thank the following: Luqman Arnold, Bob Blower, Brandon Davies, Matthew Elderfield, Michael Feeney, Desmond Fitzgerald, Bob Gumerlock, Andrew Hilton, Con Keating, Roger Kubarych, Karel Lannoo, David Lascelles, Ruben Lee, Ron Liesching, Chuck Lucas, John McPartland, Robin Munro-Davies, Maarten Nederlof, John Parry, Mike Peterson, Leslie Rahl, Neil Record, Eric Sepkes, Konstantin Graf von Schweinitz, Charles Smithson, Charles Taylor, Tim Shepheard-Walwyn and Simon Wills.

Introduction

Ships are but boordes, Saylers but men, there be land rats, and water rats, water theeues, and land theeues, I meane Pyrats, and then there is the perrill of waters, windes, and rockes.

William Shakespeare, *The Merchant of Venice*, Act I, Scene 3

Antonio's first big mistake in *The Merchant of Venice* was to bet his whole fortune on a fleet of ships; his second was to borrow 3,000 ducats from a single source. The first rule of risk management is to identify your risk. The second is to diversify it. Antonio broke the second rule, and his creditor Shylock flunked the first. He found he could not take his pound of Antonio's flesh without shedding "one drop of Christian blood": blood had not been specified as part of the bargain.

This is an unusual example. But it illustrates how financial risk management is just an extension of sensible prudence and forethought: to imagine what might go wrong and to guard against it.

Modern risk management has developed mathematics and other skills to narrow the field into bands of probabilities. It can never predict, it can only infer what might happen.

Volatility meets computer power

When did modern risk management begin? It was an extraordinary collision of extreme conditions in financial markets in the 1980s and a dramatic increase in computer power. In the space of a few years, outcomes which could be tested only by intuitive sketches on the back of an envelope, or worked out after weeks of cranky iterations on a calculator, were replicable in minutes on a desktop computer.

Monte Carlo simulations, chaos theory and neural networks have all attempted to get closer to modelling real financial markets. Of course a model will never be the real thing, and those who put too much faith in their financial model will get caught out, as the boffins at Long-Term Capital Management (a hedge fund which collapsed in 1998) spectacularly illustrated. Ultimately, even financial firms have learned that mathematics has limited value in calculating the probability of the most bizarre and extreme events.

As regulators and forward-thinking firms have got to grips with this problem, they have ventured into the more uncertain territory of designing stress-tests, imagining scenarios and occasionally playing out entire fictions of the future. This is what makes the discipline of risk management more than just a computer-driven exercise practised by nerds in back offices. It challenges the wildest imagination and the frontiers of creative genius.

Like mountain climbing, it is about minimising danger and taking calculated risks. Alpinists learn that principle fast or they and their friends die. Dealing with risk in financial markets is different: the stakes are not usually so high. And in financial markets most risktakers are risking other people's money, not their own. That makes financial markets a highly complex arena – far more complex, for instance, than a theatre of war. Every trading decision may have a plethora of motives and emotions behind it; in theory each trade adds new information, but mostly it adds noise.

In the 21st century, the noise from newswires, websites, radio, television and newspapers has become so deafening that sometimes the entire world population seems to be a single thundering herd. All humankind is focused on the troops in Afghanistan, an earthquake in Iran, the fortunes of the Dax or the Dow, or the earnings of IBM, which are "disappointing" because they did not quite surpass those in the previous quarter. Like Pavlov's dogs, we are being conditioned to salivate or recoil as massed ranks of financial news sources pump out their messages.

The limits of mathematics

Good financial risktakers have to make sense of all this garbage. And they have to combat their own emotions, because dealing in financial markets, even on others' behalf, is an emotional business. Even if they are not your own dreams, you are seeing people's dreams made or unmade every day. Money, or wealth, especially these days, is the chief means through which people hope to enhance their lives. So the financial markets, apart from being a vital clearing mechanism for world commerce, are places of dreams and emotions. Someone who takes that on board will never make the mistake of believing that market behaviour can be mimicked by maths.

Despite that caveat, a whole industry has grown up in the last 30 years based on the idea that the behaviour of financial markets can be interpreted and outsmarted by mathematical models. The modelmakers sell the illusion that patterns and prices will repeat themselves. Sometimes the illusion is self-fulfilling.

The endless fascination of markets is that they are always changing, as if consciously seeking to spite human efforts to tame them. Just as fascinating is the behaviour of the institutions that make up the markets: banks, investment banks, insurance companies, corporate treasuries, brokers, exchanges, clearing houses, central banks, pension funds, hedge funds, day-traders and speculators. Like strings of mountain climbers they are keen to safeguard their own survival. But to stay in the game they have to take risks.

Calculated financial risktaking, and the way in which institutions align themselves to do it, is the most compelling game of all and the underlying subject of this book. Individual investors and speculators make mistakes and they can lose their shirts. But financial institutions are like battleships: a mistake by one of the crew rarely sinks the ship – Nick Leeson's rogue trading at Barings in 1995 being an exception. Nevertheless, an institution must be run in a disciplined enough way, not only to avoid destruction but also to be an effective fighting machine and score victories.

Employees of financial firms are not usually amenable to military discipline, although some managers have tried. Handling deal-hungry investment bankers – probably the greatest management challenge of all – has been compared with herding cats or squirrels.

Trials and errors

More fascinating than risk-management successes, which are generally non-events, are the spectacular failures. Failures tell us about the extremes of financial stress. There are plenty of lessons to be learned from the collapses of Barings, Metallgesellschaft, Long-Term Capital Management and other lesser blips, many of which are analysed in this book. Such analysis should help prevent financial institutions from making the same mistake twice. But this has not always been the case, as some rather accident-prone institutions have shown.

This book considers the notion that dealing with financial risk, however serious and grown-up it seems, is nevertheless a game. It has basic rules and set pieces, and performance that can be improved by practice. Yet most risk managers and the institutions they work for – and indeed those who regulate them – do not give themselves the chance to test their skills in practice; they are generally at the coal-face doing it for real 24 hours a day.

Learning from past mistakes is useful. Learning from the mistakes that could happen tomorrow is a crucial risk-management exercise. Yet the little scenario-building and stress-testing that financial institutions have done so far is mostly too abstract. They do not expose their staff in training to the kinds of stresses that occur in live financial crises. But they could, and should, do so at little extra cost, by playing full-blooded financial war games, internally and even with rival institutions. The case for role-playing and crisis simulations is put in Chapter 12.

1

FINANCIAL RISK: AN ENDLESS CHALLENGE

1 The growth of modern financial markets

In October 1973 Egypt and Syria lost the Yom Kippur war against Israel. But soon afterwards the Arab states learned the true power of another weapon that they had at their disposal: oil. Provided they stuck together and limited their production, the Middle Eastern members of the Organisation of Petroleum Exporting Countries (OPEC) had enough embargo power to drive up the price of crude oil worldwide.

In November 1973 the price of oil rose from $4 a barrel to $22 a barrel as OPEC's embargo took effect. Petrol rationing was introduced in America and Britain. The embargo lasted nine months and the scarcity of petroleum products triggered rounds of price increases affecting almost every item that needed transporting, including food, newspapers, clothing and household goods. Soon inflation was galloping along nicely on both sides of the Atlantic.

The other driver of inflation was the hugely increased revenue that the OPEC states earned from the high oil price. The dollars had to go somewhere. With such volumes there was only one option, to deposit them with the world's biggest international banks. Banks are not in the habit of refusing deposits, but sometimes they have trouble putting the deposits to work.

Petrodollar recycling

By more than a coincidence, the world's big banks began to develop a business which could use these huge volumes of cash: making balance-of-payments loans to the governments of developing countries. In those days there was a popular assumption that governments did not go bust, since, rather than default on their debts, they could simply borrow more money from their citizens. On this basis, billions of recycled petrodollars were lent by syndicates of banks to the governments of Mexico, Brazil, Peru, Venezuela and Turkey and also to states behind the Iron Curtain: Poland, Romania, Hungary and the Soviet Union.

An international financial market developed in which huge amounts of dollars were lent at floating rates of interest to many countries whose national currency tended naturally to devalue against the dollar –

although there was often a barrier to devaluation in the form of exchange controls.

Turkey is one example of a country that ran into trouble. In October 1973 there was a general election, the first since the army took political control two years earlier following a spate of extremist violence. There was no clear election winner and Bulent Ecevit, the head of the social democrats, took nearly six weeks to build a shaky coalition. This was not a time to undermine the nation's morale further by devaluing the currency or putting up the price of essential goods such as sugar and petrol, both of which were scarce. Somehow Turkey managed to maintain its exchange rate at TL14 to the dollar, and petrol prices at the pumps were kept stubbornly low. But sooner or later something had to give.

Turkey was running a big current-account deficit with the help of foreign bank loans and deposits sent home by migrant workers in western Europe. To attract hard currency, the Turkish central bank had to pay well above the prevailing market interest rates for dollars and D-marks. As the Turkish government lurched from crisis to crisis – the invasion of Cyprus in July 1974, new elections in September and another long delay before the next coalition was formed – it had increasing difficulty attracting foreign currency loans.

Too good to be true

In 1975, in desperation, the central bank devised a new kind of foreign-currency deposit, which protected foreign investors from a future devaluation of the Turkish lira. The convertible Turkish lira deposit account paid high Turkish lira interest rates and, at maturity, promised to make good any difference resulting from the lira's devaluation against the dollar (or sterling, D-marks and Swiss francs). In other words, you could invest dollars at Turkish lira interest rates (around 9% at the time). The deposits were renewable every three months. For those who spotted this amazing "risk-free" offer, it seemed a great opportunity to make a killing at the Turkish government's expense. Convertible lira deposits boomed, and the Turkish government was able to continue its unrealistic spending spree, including subsidising imports of sugar and petrol.

Of course it could not last. The government found it increasingly difficult to repay depositors in full when they asked to withdraw their hard cash. The political situation was also deteriorating. In 1977 Turkey declared a moratorium on its foreign debt. The convertible lira accounts were frozen and rescheduled, along with all of Turkey's other foreign loans. Depositors who had not got their money out earlier found that their three-month deposits had become involuntary seven-year loans at a much reduced rate of interest.

The Turkish default did not have much impact on the career path of a new breed of international banker, the loan syndication officer, who was rewarded for lending billions of dollars at increasingly high interest rates to governments around the world. The risk of almost any sovereign government was acceptable, since the countries were thought unlikely to repudiate their debts. Kenya, Uganda, Ivory Coast, Jamaica and even Haiti put themselves in hock to these providers of plenty at the stroke of a Mont Blanc pen. No government of whatever political complexion in whatever struggling country, big or small, was neglected until it had its own multimillion-dollar loan facility from the world's greatest banks: Citibank, Chemical Bank, First Chicago, Manufacturers Hanover, Lloyds Bank, Deutsche Bank, to name just a few.

Chicago rules

In the early 1980s two new forces hit financial markets. First, western industrial economies, racked by five years of inflation, began to address their problems by raising domestic interest rates. The remedy was dubbed Reaganomics, after America's president, Ronald Reagan, who applied it on the advice of Chicago School "supply-side" economists, such as Milton Friedman and Friedrich Hayek. Reaganomics was copied in Britain by Margaret Thatcher, the prime minister, and to some extent by the German Bundesbank. Dollar interest rates screamed up to 22%.

Second, the countries that had borrowed all the petrodollars were finding it increasingly difficult to service their foreign-currency debt. Commodity prices were low (apart from oil), world trade was shrinking, and the interest component of their debt was becoming far higher than they had anticipated. In central Europe, the governments of Poland and Romania defaulted on their bank debt. Hungary narrowly missed the same fate. In September 1982 came the shock announcement that Mexico was halting payments on its external debt.

This was followed by a decade of defaults by more developing countries, including Brazil, the biggest. In each case there was a stand-off between the debtor and its creditors – which were mostly banks – until the debt was rescheduled. Walter Wriston, the chairman of Citicorp, had once said reassuringly that countries do not go bust. He was right. But they can default on their debt, and they can suffer horribly from the results of overborrowing and then refusing or delaying payments, which hurts the lenders too.

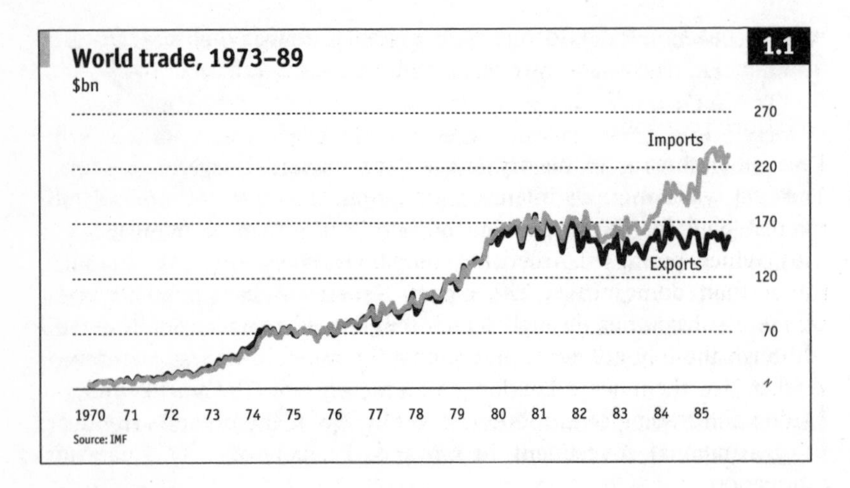

As a result of sovereign debt negotiations, techniques were developed that allowed the loans to be transferred and traded. This made it easier for banks that wanted to cut their losses and sell their credit exposure to another bank at a knockdown price. Once the trading of discounted debt became common, it was possible for countries to secure some real reduction of their debt burden, either by buying back the debt at a discount, or by repackaging it as a new form of debt on better terms. The route taken by many countries was to repackage the bank loans as bonds, with a guaranteed repayment of principal at the end of the bonds' life – so-called Brady bonds. Lenders liked the reduction of their overall exposure and the fact that the bonds were easily tradable. It meant that other investors besides banks could come in as buyers. It also meant that a future default by the country would be far more complex, involving thousands of individual bondholders, not just a handful of banks. It was thought that the conversion of bank loans into Brady bonds would severely discourage countries from defaulting again.

Brady bonds, and other bond issues by developing or "emerging-market" countries, became a huge new asset class. By the mid-1990s there were around $190 billion of Brady bonds and perhaps $500 billion of other emerging-market bonds outstanding, mostly on the books of banks but also owned by investment institutions and specialist emerging-market funds.

In around 20 years the world of international finance had changed from one in which loans for countries and international corporations were predominantly raised domestically, and were driven by the borrower's need for cash, to one with a great interweaving of financial flows, including cash, derivatives, discounted loans and securities.

Offshore freedom

Two other threads of history shaped the modern financial markets. The first was America's interest equalisation tax (a tax of 15% on the interest paid by foreign issuers of bonds in America), imposed in 1963, which prompted American companies to issue bonds offshore rather than domestically. The biggest American companies formed offshore subsidiaries through which they issued so-called Eurobonds. Although these bonds were predominantly issued in dollars, the main markets for them were London and Luxembourg. The underwriting, issuing and trading of Eurobonds became one of the pivotal activities of international investment banks and a laboratory for financial innovation.

The second was America's decision in 1971 to end the dollar's link with the gold standard. The exchange rate of the dollar was allowed to float freely. In a few years, foreign-exchange trading and speculation had become a huge activity for banks. But the mechanics of forex trading changed little to take account of the increased volumes and the increased exposure to exchange-rate fluctuations. A wake-up call came in July 1974 when a German bank, Bankhaus Herstatt, was closed down before the end of the American business day. It had collected payments in yen, D-marks and other European currencies, but failed to honour its dollar payments in New York. This caused gridlock in the foreign-exchange markets, as banks panicked and refused to release payments for other perfectly sound transactions. The small Herstatt bankruptcy had worldwide repercussions, demonstrating how fast contagion could spread through the world financial system.

Stockmarkets have always been volatile, but such volatility in currencies, interest rates, bonds and even loan prices was something new. With so many new variables it was becoming increasingly important for companies and banks to find ways of protecting themselves against extreme fluctuations. This simple need gave birth to a highly complex activity: the creation, selling and trading of financial derivatives.

Off-balance-sheet games

Stock and commodity futures had already been traded for almost a century. For some time, banks had provided forward foreign-exchange contracts to help customers hedge payments receivable or payable in other currencies. But apart from the increase in market variables, three phenomena stimulated the growth of complex derivatives.

- The increase in computer power. This allowed complex financial calculations involving many variables and many iterations to be done in minutes or seconds. Moore's law, which holds that computing power doubles every 18 months in relation to its cost, was as much a driver as the underlying need. Computers were creating their own extra work in financial derivatives.
- The swap. This simple innovation, almost a sleight of hand, changed the face of financial markets. The earliest swaps were actually "back-to-back" loans. Because of currency restrictions, a company in one country wanting to raise money in the currency of another would find a company in that country in a similar position. Each company would borrow in its domestic market; then the two companies would exchange the proceeds and continue to service each other's loans. The swap, developed in around 1980, stripped that concept to its essence, which was a netting of two different cash flows – such as a fixed rate of interest and a floating rate of interest – on the same notional amount of money. The positive net difference at each interest period is paid to one counterparty or the other. The two cash flows could be based in different currencies, such as dollars and D-marks, in which case the net difference payable would take account of how the exchange rate had moved since the initiation of the swap. (See Figures 1.2 and 1.3.)

  Once the concept of the swap was understood, it could be applied to any pair of cash flows, independent of any underlying loan or bond issue. There could be a swap agreement, for example, to pay or receive the net difference in cash flows between the performance of the Dow Jones Industrial Average and fluctuations in the price of gold, or oil, or Mexican government bonds. But the swap's biggest use has been for interest-rate hedging or speculation. By the late 1990s around $10 trillion in notional amounts of swaps were being written annually.
- The growth of financial futures exchanges. Commodity futures have been traded for centuries, but the demand for futures contracts on three-month dollar interest rates was recognised after the extreme fluctuations of the early 1980s. The Chicago

1.2 Three-month dollar interest rates and volatility (Riskgrade), 1971–2003

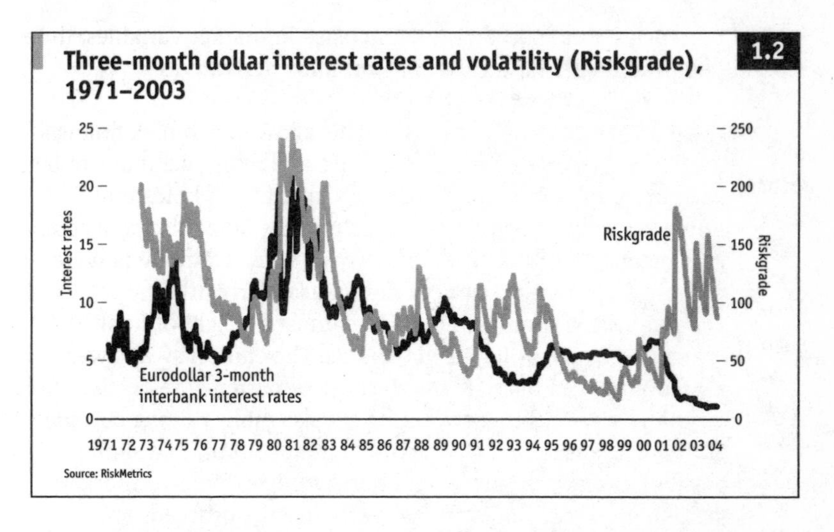

Source: RiskMetrics

Mercantile Exchange launched the first cash-settled financial futures contract on dollar interest rates in 1981, after which other contracts were soon launched on Treasury bonds, various currencies and the S&P 500 stock index. These soon became essential tools for hedging risks incurred in the over-the-counter markets. Standardised, liquid instruments traded on exchanges were used to offset positions in the assets traded bilaterally, such as Treasury bonds, equities and foreign exchange. The cross-

1.3 The dollar exchange rate and its volatility (Riskgrade) against the D-mark (1971–99) and the euro (1999–2003)

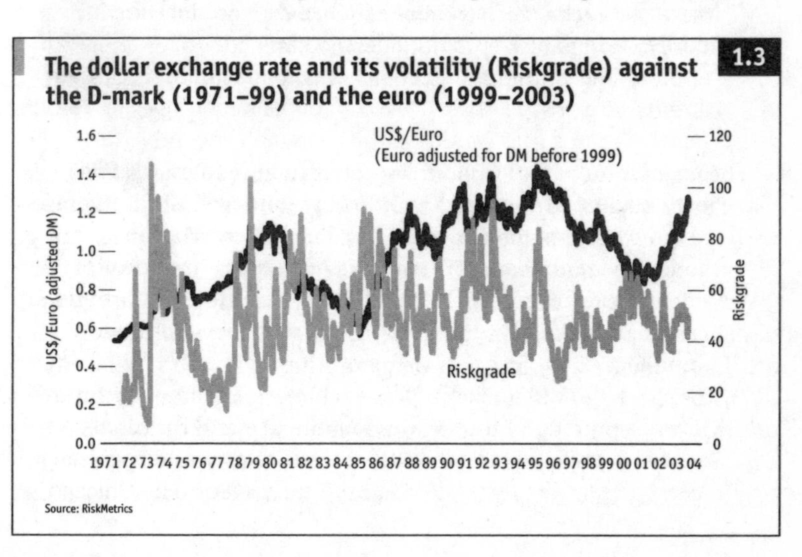

Source: RiskMetrics

Table 1.1 **Growth in volume of the swap market, 1987–2002 (outstanding notional amounts, $bn)**

	Interest-rate swaps	*Cross-currency swaps*
1987	683	183
1988	1,010	317
1989	1,503	435
1990	2,312	578
1991	3,065	807
1992	3,851	860
1993	6,177	900
1994	8,816	915
1995	12,811	1,197
1996	19,171	1,560
1997	22,291	1,824
1998	36,262	2,253
1999	43,936	2,444
2000	48,768	3,194
2001	58,897	3,942
2002	79,120	4,903

Sources: International Swaps and Derivatives Association (ISDA); Bank for International Settlements

trading of exchange-listed and off-exchange products led financial companies to a more detailed breakdown or "unbundling" of these risks, mostly market risks, into their component parts.

The logical outcome of unbundling, taken to its extreme, is that every risk can be separated out, priced and sold in the market to the buyer with the greatest appetite for it. In this way the world's risks can be redistributed for maximum efficiency: the risktakers are rewarded and the risk-averse can sleep at night. But this is rather idealistic and impractical. In the real world, risks cannot be completely unbundled, since they are intertwined. Every financial bargain brings with it a multiplicity of risks, not just the risk that market prices will fluctuate. There is the credit risk that the counterparty to the transaction will not keep its side of the bargain; there is the operational risk that the transaction will not be processed correctly; and there are the many other risks, such as legal and reputational risk, that can affect the value of a bargain and a party's ability to honour it or continue in business. It is almost impossible to identify all these risks, let alone to quantify, unbundle and price them separately.

But in the two decades from around 1982 to 2002, financial institutions spent a great deal of their energy and resources trying to do just that, encouraged by regulators. Little energy and resources were spent, for better or worse, on trying to redesign the financial environment to make it less risky. Natural evolution was the order of the day, driven by the major players in the financial arena.

2 Market theory

A cynic knows the price of everything and the value of nothing.

Oscar Wilde

By this definition, a cynic would be a good options trader.

From the moment you are born you are faced with options, in other words choices. You can choose to smile or cry, to get drunk and fall off your bicycle or take the train. An option is the right, but not the obligation, to take a course of action. A financial option (see box opposite) may allow you to settle a contract at an opportune moment, to buy a security at a certain price, to pay off a loan, or to refinance your house. Every option, in theory, has a price, even an option not to go to the cinema – roughly, this would be the cost of the ticket and the meal afterwards, minus the pleasure the film would have given you, weighed against the chore of cooking dinner and washing up.

Financial options try to be a little more scientific, but it is worth bearing in mind that no option has an absolute ascertainable value. All option pricing depends on an accepted convention or formula.

Take an option to buy a share. A company's shares are trading at $24. You have an option for which you paid $2 a month ago to buy a share at $26, at any time over the next 11 months. What is its value if you wanted to sell that option in the market today? It depends on how probable it is that the company's shares will exceed the strike price of your option plus the price you sell the option for.

Logically, you would say it depends on the future performance of the company. But option theorists do not work that way. They have learned enough about the ups and downs of stockmarkets to believe that the most important factor is the volatility of the company's share price, and the volatility of the market in general. This, anyway, has come to be the accepted principle for pricing options.

The most famous formula for calculating the price of an option is Black-Scholes. Even Fischer Black and Myron Scholes, the devisers of the formula, admitted that it is a flawed approximation of the real world. John Cox, Stephen Ross, Mark Rubinstein and others later added refinements, but the formulas are still only as good as the assumptions that are fed into them about the volatility of the market and the cost of trading. In the end, the price of an option depends on the sentiment of the buyer and the seller, maybe even on what they had for breakfast.

Options and option pricing, however uncertain and flawed, are a fundamental building-block of financial risk management.

How options work

An option is the right, but not the obligation, to buy or sell something, for instance a block of shares, at a set price at a future date. The perceived value of the option today varies according to views of what the market price of those shares will be when the option is exercised. If it is an option to buy, it will increase in value as the share price increases and have zero value if the share price falls below the exercise price, and is expected to stay there through the life of the option. If it is an option to sell, it will rise in value as the share price falls and have zero value if the share price rises above the exercise price, and is expected to stay there through the life of the option. Options, therefore, can be extremely useful as a means of taking a position, either to hedge or to speculate, without buying or selling the underlying instrument, whether it is shares, bonds, a commodity, foreign exchange, or a right to borrow or lend at a certain interest rate.

Buying an option carries a limited risk of loss (the cost of the option if it expires worthless) and a chance of (theoretically) unlimited gain as the strike price and the price of the underlying instrument diverge in the option's favour. The greater the divergence the more the option is said to be "in the money". For example, if the holder has bought an option to buy a share at $3 and the market price of the share is $5, the option is $2 in the money. If the share price is $2, the option is $1 out of the money.

The option seller is in the opposite and far more dangerous position. There is a limited chance of gain – the option premium – if the option expires worthless, but there is the risk of (theoretically) unlimited loss, depending on how far the option is in the money. Options sellers take this risk because they calculate that on aggregate they will take in more premium than they will lose from buyers exercising their options. They price the options according to these calculations.

But how can such a price be calculated scientifically? After all, it is a price based on the future direction that a market price will take, and no one has yet invented a machine that sees into the future. The answer is that it cannot be totally scientific. Every attempt at finding the present value of an option, or indeed the present value of anything at a future date, is a fudge.

However, the fudgers have become pretty good at their job. Professional option sellers are generally confident that they can take more premium than the losses they incur, rather like insurance underwriters.

The premium price is often based on a mathematical model, such as the Black-Scholes formula. It is important to remember that Black-Scholes and all other mathematical models are only an approximation of reality. The models are only as good as the data and assumptions that are fed into them, and option pricing depends heavily on a view of future market volatility.

The price at which options are bought and sold depends partly on these pricing models but also, like any other traded instrument, on the force of supply and demand. Option prices can often diverge sharply from the observed volatility in the market, perhaps because one trader has a contrarian view, or because herd behaviour, and a clamour to buy or sell, drives the price up or down.

Lastly, it must be remembered that there is no absolutely right price for an option: it embodies a view of the future which could be either right or wrong.

Risk managers try to price everything. Even a transaction – or course of action – forgone has an "opportunity cost", so that can be priced too.

Option theory has been extended to the world of business risk, such as decisions on whether or not to build a factory or, having decided to build one, whether to build it in China or Indonesia. These are called "real" options. It has also been applied, or misapplied, to the valuation of fishery conservation. In this case an option value was assigned to the effect that conservation has on reducing the uncertainty of fish catches and hence the volatility in the price. The model showed that the price paid for conservation was well below the cost of buying an option to hedge the fish price – a spurious way of proving that conservation is good even for fishermen.

Risk versus reward

The measure of risk against reward is a central exercise in assessing the performance of an investment fund, or the performance of any financial asset. It is all very well to scan the markets for investments that promise a high return, such as junk bonds or Peruvian railway shares, but the riskiness of an asset usually bears some relation to the return it offers. The most common measure of riskiness against return is the Sharpe ratio, a formula that relates volatility of price (the violence with which it fluctuates up or down) to actual return. Named after William Sharpe, a professor at Stanford University's Graduate School of Business and a subsequent Nobel prizewinner, the Sharpe ratio has its flaws and critics too, since past prices are not exactly a measure of future

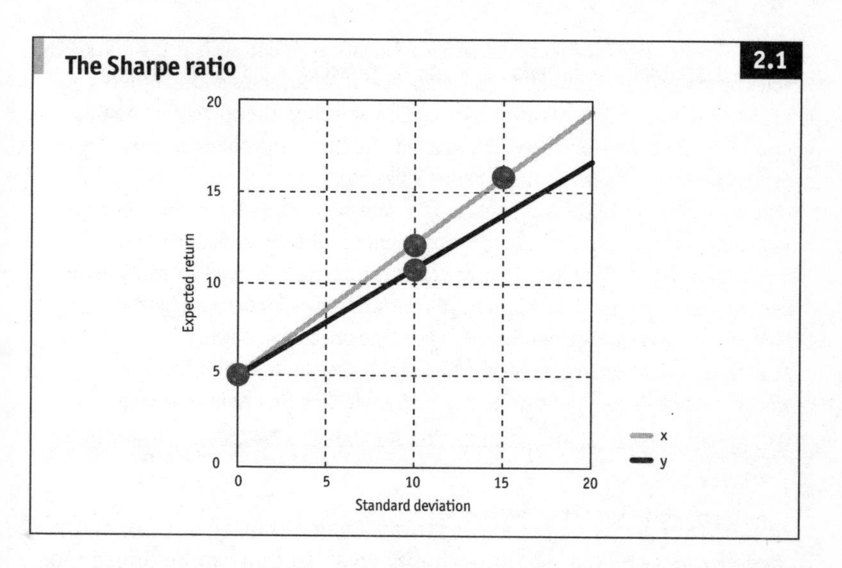

performance. Once again, approximations have to suffice in a science that can only test itself against empirical evidence, not elegant proofs.

X and Y are two mutual funds. The following explanation was written by William Sharpe himself:

> *Consider an investor who plans to put all her money in either fund X or fund Y. Moreover, assume that the graph plots the best possible predictions of future expected return and future risk, measured by the standard deviation of return. She might choose X, based on its higher expected return, despite its greater risk. Or she might choose Y, based on its lower risk, despite its lower expected return. Her choice should depend on her tolerance for accepting risk in pursuit of higher expected return. Absent some knowledge of her preferences, an outside analyst cannot argue that X is better than Y or the converse.*

Whereas the Sharpe ratio deals with the potential risk of loss in a portfolio compared with its gain, Omega, developed by Con Keating and William Shadwick, looks at the potential for higher gain compared with performance. In other words, Omega bases investment choices on risk appetite and a loss-tolerance threshold rather than risk aversion. On paper it seems as well based mathematically as the Sharpe ratio as a guide to risk and return, but to the cautious mind it also seems dangerous.

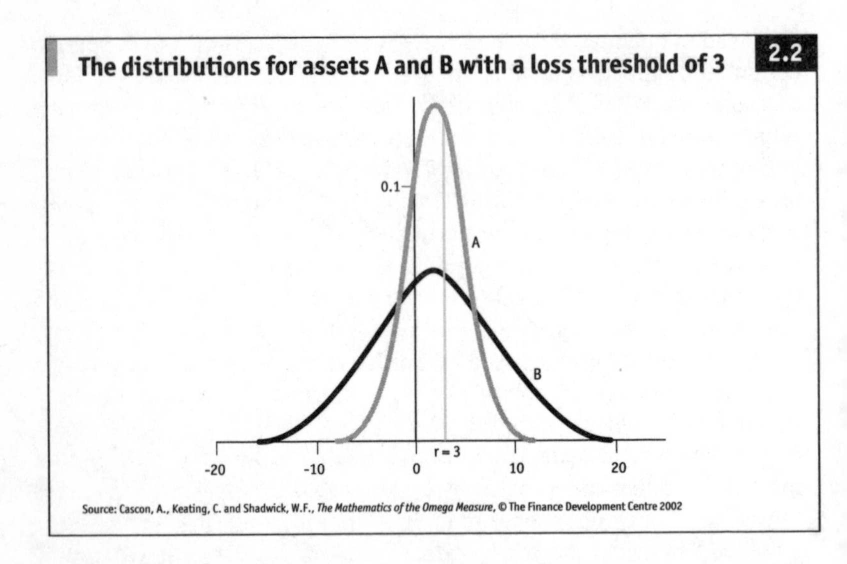

2.2 The distributions for assets A and B with a loss threshold of 3

Source: Cascon, A., Keating, C. and Shadwick, W.F., *The Mathematics of the Omega Measure*, © The Finance Development Centre 2002

Figure 2.2 shows gain and loss distribution curves for assets A and B. The risk-averse Sharpe ratio would always favour A. But Omega argues that if you have a high risk appetite, and your target is to make returns of over 3 (where the vertical line is), then B is a better bet (because it has a larger area than A to the right of the vertical line).

Market wizards

Finding patterns in markets and extrapolating future patterns from the past have fascinated market watchers over the centuries. Even before computers, chartists used historical data as a means of spotting trends and following them. As computing power increased, the pattern seekers were tempted to process ever greater volumes of market data in the quest for hitherto undetected patterns that might make a trader's fortune. In general, this quest seems to be self-defeating. Future market behaviour is so complex and uncertain that it cannot be extrapolated from past events. However, this has not discouraged certain market wizards from taking advantage of trends in the very short term on the basis of recognisably repeated patterns.

Doyne Farmer and Norman Packard at the Santa Fe Institute in New Mexico were among the first to try to apply non-linear equations from chaos theory to financial markets. It appears that they had little success with chaos theory but more with the application of raw computer power. Their financial careers began in 1981, when for a while they managed to outsmart a roulette wheel in Las Vegas using a toe-operated computer strapped to a shoe. Their adventures are recorded in a book, *The Eudaemonic Pie.*[1] In 1991 they formed the Prediction Company, which aimed to beat financial markets with the use of neural networks and other computer-aided learning techniques. A year later they signed an exclusive agreement with O'Connor & Associates, a Chicago-based derivatives trading firm (now part of UBS). By their own account, Prediction Company has consistently made money and is still expanding into new markets, although Farmer and Packard left after a decade to pursue other areas of scientific interest.

Many other computer-based groups have sought to use pattern recognition to follow and jump ahead of market trends. Such techniques are suited to very short-term trading, but the frequency of trades means that most of the profit is eaten up in transaction costs. It is a fact of life that market anomalies that provide astute traders with unusually big excess returns are ironed out sooner or later, so that their returns are eroded.

Market bets that are longer-term, based on fundamental economic observations, sometimes make the investor or speculator a large amount of money. But again, the world picture on the basis of which the trader is trading seldom persists for long, and the trader who once seemed infallible turns out to have feet of clay. A good example is George Soros, whose honest book *The Alchemy of Finance*[2] documents how, during 14 months of reasonably successful trading in major currencies and stockmarkets, he nevertheless is walloped by the Japanese stockmarket, failing to get out in time. Soros is regarded as one of the most astute macroeconomic investors, but his reputation rests on one or two big wins, for example against sterling in 1992. *The Alchemy of Finance* contains an admission by Soros:

> *My financial success stands in stark contrast with my ability to forecast events ... The best that can be said for it is that my theoretical framework enables me to understand the significance of events as they unfold.*

The theory of efficient markets, which says that markets in which complete information is uniformly shared will provide no more than an average return, is clearly not borne out by experience. All markets are more or less inefficient, and the information that motivates trades is incomplete and unfairly shared.

This has not prevented efficient market theory from being an extremely useful tool for the allocation of investments. If nothing else, it reminds those who believe they can outsmart the market that they will not do so for long, unless of course they have inside information.

The foundation of this approach is CAPM, the capital asset pricing model, developed by William Sharpe in the 1960s (he won a Nobel prize in 1990 for his work on this and the Sharpe ratio). CAPM sees the risk of an investment portfolio as being dependent on two things: fluctuations in the entire market; and fluctuations in individual stock prices because of individual company news. Provided a portfolio is sufficiently diversified, Sharpe argues, all the investor needs to worry about is the market risk, or "beta".

Risk managers have always to bear in mind that markets do not produce abnormal excess returns in the long run. The trick, it seems, is to get in or out before the beginning or end of a trend. In 1999, a 15-year bull market came to an end. People who had been predicting its end for five years or more were at last able to say "I told you so"; but where, over those five years, had they been making money?

Enduring heroes

Airport bookstalls and business libraries are full of volumes by or about market traders and how they made their millions. There is an endless fascination in such literature, as there is in watching lottery shows and *Who wants to be a millionaire*. *Market Wizards*,[3] by Jack Schwager, contains a series of interviews with some of the world's leading financial traders. Each trader in the book is there, and not history, because of a factor called "survivor bias". If his run of success had been short, he would not be there. So thousands of other potential market wizards who could have been in the book eliminated themselves by a run of bad luck.

However, the tales of experienced traders are always a good read because these people expose themselves to extremes: in this case the glee of winning and the agony of losing. The best of them have managed to master these emotions, which are the enemy of successful trading. The markets themselves are as much the aggregate of sentiment and emotion as they are of fundamental data. Those who succumb to the sentiment, it seems, usually end up as the market's victims.

3 Derivatives and leverage

In September 1992 the cover of *Euromoney*, a well-known financial magazine, had a picture of green creatures mixing gruesome potions, presumably to feed to unsuspecting humans. The cover story was about derivatives and the damage that they could do to financial firms, or their customers, if they were not used correctly.

This sensational view of derivatives enraged the financial community at the time. Derivatives sellers had taken a great deal of time and trouble to explain to their customers how these instruments, correctly used, are powerful tools that can improve financial performance, only to have that hard work dashed to pieces by the financial magazine's unkind words. *Euromoney*, the so-called "journal of the world's capital markets", was supposed to be the financial dealer's friend.

Euromoney was right; the salesmen were wrong. Derivatives cannot come with enough health warnings. The reason is their ability to accelerate gains or losses, often for little initial outlay.

Derivatives, as their name suggests, are derived from an underlying asset, or an index representing assets. They are not assets themselves, although they can be traded as if they have an underlying value. So, for example, warrants to buy Volkswagen shares at a certain price three months from now will trade at a price related to the underlying shares, but supply and demand will also give the price of the warrants a life of its own. Buying warrants is a cheap way of getting exposure to a share, with the risk of loss limited to the cost of the warrants. A few dollars or euros spent initially have the chance of being multiplied many times if the share price rises; this is more exciting than, say, the return on a fixed interest government bond.

A zero-sum game

But there is another side to the tale. In the derivatives market, for every winner there is a loser. The sellers of such warrants suffer an accelerated loss, or an opportunity cost, as the share price rises. If they are sensible, the sellers will have covered themselves by owning the underlying shares in question – they will have written a so-called "covered" call option. When the warrant is cashed in they simply hand over the shares in their possession at the agreed price. They have lost an opportunity to make money, but not their shirts.

For experienced dealers in derivatives, however, selling covered calls, or covered warrants, is not the most interesting activity. They prefer to rely on their ability to judge how much of their position they must hedge, for example by buying some of the underlying assets, or by selling part of their position to owners of such assets, or by investing in related futures.

These are simple derivatives, whose behaviour is well known. But the history of the derivatives market, which took off in the early 1980s, is littered with accidents which happened because one or other party to the bargain, or both, did not properly anticipate the behaviour of the derivative and the legal, or documentary, or profit-and-loss implications.

Take interest-rate swaps, introduced in Chapter 1. Some of the early swaps had rather primitive documentation. Careful documentation is necessary because swaps, unlike most other financial contracts, rely on the performance of both counterparties, rather than just one. This is because, with a net exchange of cash flows, at each interest period a payment of the net difference could be due from either one counterparty or the other. Because of this two-sided credit risk, each party has documentary protection against the other's default and can terminate the contract if certain conditions are not met. In the early days, when there were few swaps outstanding, the primitive documentation allowed some counterparties to terminate their swap agreements on the slightest pretext, such as a name change or change of ownership. Moreover, with this kind of early agreement, because of a clause stipulating "limited two-way payments", if one counterparty went into default, even if it had a swap position with a positive value, it could not claim the money owed on the swap.

Reading the small print

There were several celebrated instances of this. For example, in 1987, Texaco, an oil company, technically went bankrupt for a few days when ordered to pay $10.5 billion in damages in a wrangle over the purchase of Getty Oil. Bankers Trust, a big American bank, saw the opportunity to terminate a swap agreement with Texaco on which, because of the movement of interest and currency rates since it was signed, it would have had to pay Texaco an estimated $10m over its remaining life. Texaco, having insisted on its own documentation in the first place, was considered fair game; Bankers Trust walked off with a windfall profit.

The International Swap Dealers Association (ISDA, later called the

International Swaps and Derivatives Association), which had devised the standard swap documentation, tried to change the limited two-way payments clause to a more sophisticated version, called "full two-way payments", which encouraged swap counterparties to net all their swap agreements in the case of a default. This would mean that even if a swap counterparty was in default, it could claim credit for swap agreements in which interest or exchange rates had moved in its favour and offset their net present value against its other obligations.

Most swap practitioners recognised that the full two-way payments principle was necessary for a smooth functioning of the market. This was aptly demonstrated in 1989, with the bankruptcy of Development Finance Corporation of New Zealand. Most of DFC's counterparties agreed to net out all their swap agreements, in the interests of an orderly unwinding of DFC's swaps. But there were some notable exceptions, including the Australian subsidiary of Security Pacific, an American bank, which, like Bankers Trust in the previous example, would have owed DFC about $7m. SecPac decided to exercise its legal right, under the limited two-way payments clause, to walk away from its obligations. SecPac may have saved itself some money, but it was a pariah in the derivative community until 1992, when it agreed to pay DFC $3m in an out-of-court settlement.

Rotten boroughs

Derivatives have also fallen foul of the law. The most celebrated case is the London Borough of Hammersmith & Fulham, which like some other British boroughs became an active user of interest-rate swaps. If properly used by municipal treasurers, interest-rate swaps can tailor interest-rate risk to a council's income and payment liabilities. But some British boroughs in the mid-1980s began to use swaps, and options on swaps, as a way to gamble on interest rates to make profits. The finance director of Hammersmith & Fulham and his colleagues exposed the borough to the risk that interest rates would rise by entering swap and cap transactions. They also sold swaptions, which are options to enter a swap agreement at a set rate at some time in the future. Because they believed that interest rates would continue to fall, they sold swaptions that would be out of the money if they did indeed fall. Unfortunately, interest rates rose and Hammersmith & Fulham soon faced a big loss. The borough continued to gamble, in the vain hope of recouping its losses. The audit commission, which oversees municipal finances, spotted the problem and ruled that the finance director and his colleagues had acted *ultra vires*, or outside their official powers. Several banks brought a court action to assert their contracted rights. They lost in the first instance, then won on appeal, but lost ultimately in the House of Lords. The law lords ruled that all municipal treasurers who had made swap agreements had acted beyond their powers. All swap contracts with municipalities in Britain were declared null and void.

It was a terrible blow to the still-young swap fraternity. But it was also a salutary lesson: that a counterparty in a complex derivatives contract must ensure that both signatories have the power to commit to the agreement. Thereafter, everyone in the swap community knew the meaning of the Latin expression *ultra vires*.

The history of derivatives, indeed any kind of new financial instrument, is one of experiment, invention and selling initially with a wide profit margin, which then erodes as the product becomes less exotic and more of a commodity. It happened with swaps, interest-rate caps and securitised mortgages, and later with equity and credit derivatives.

Pride comes before a fall

Often, reliance on home-grown risk modelling has led to significant losses, followed by a rethink of the business. Merrill Lynch, an American investment bank, for example, lost $400m in the early 1980s on securitised mortgages. With mortgage securitisation, a pool of home loans is sliced into tranches bearing different degrees of risk. Some tranches rely only on the mortgagee's interest payments, whereas others rely on repayment of principal. These interest-only and principal-only tranches had very different loss experiences under different market conditions. If a large proportion of mortgages in the pool are repaid early, the interest-only tranche suffers a drastic fall in value. Along with other American investment banks, Merrill Lynch had made wrong assumptions about the loss rate in the interest-only pool. They had not realised how volatile returns could be for this part of the mortgage product.

In 1988, Chemical Bank became the leading marketmaker in interest-rate caps. (Caps are a form of insurance against a floating interest rate rising above a certain level.) The seller of a cap promises to pay the extra cost if interest rates exceed the strike level of the cap. Caps at that time were a new product, and providers of caps, mostly banks, were cautious about pricing them. After all, they were similar to an option: the cap would cost the provider money if interest rates breached a certain level. That likelihood depended on the volatility of interest rates and, of course, on macroeconomic factors such as inflationary pressure and the use of interest-rate hikes to control it. Chemical Bank devised its own cap pricing formula and fed it with volatility assumptions, which allowed it to sell caps more cheaply and more aggressively than the rest of the market. For a while, other cap dealers were flabbergasted and wondered how the bank could be so aggressive. But after re-examining their own risk models they decided that it was underestimating the risk. Brave Chemical Bank became a provider of caps to the entire market until, rather inevitably, a rise in interest rates triggered payments on many cap agreements. The margin the bank had charged on its deals failed to cover its losses of around $30m.

Dangerous assumptions

Getting volatility assumptions wrong is a classic risk-management failure. Ultimately, it is more a failure of management than of mathematics, since every mathematical model has to be fed with assumptions input by humans. Models can always be manipulated either deliberately or mistakenly by those who are applying them. It is up to managers and risk controllers to weed out these aberrations before they do damage.

NatWest Markets, the short-lived investment banking arm of Britain's National Westminster Bank, exposed itself to losses on long-dated interest-rate options because its risk managers ignored what is known as the "volatility smile". The smile is the degree to which an option pricing model can move out of line at the far edges of probability, when there is little trading information to go on, either because such options are traded only rarely, or because they have a long maturity. In such cases the model's pricing must constantly be checked against both the common sense of an experienced trader and a stress-test to show what would happen in extreme conditions. NatWest's risk managers failed to do this and lost around £80m ($130m) in 1997 after their volatility assumptions proved too optimistic.

Union Bank of Switzerland (UBS) had a similar experience in 1997 with equity derivatives. Its equity derivatives team in New York and Singapore had been aggressively selling derivatives that protected buyers for up to seven years against falls in various stockmarket indexes or individual shares. There are several ways in which it could have hedged such a position. The safest way would have been to sell futures (run a short position) in the relevant equity indexes, so that if share prices fell its loss on the equity derivatives would be made good by its gain on the futures. But such a hedge could only be short-term (futures contracts are not liquid beyond one year and are expensive to renew), whereas the equity derivatives contracts had maturities of several years. UBS used the less expensive but riskier technique of dynamic or delta hedging. Depending on how much its derivative positions moved out of the money, it would sell a calculated amount of futures to limit its loss. Dynamic hedging relies on prompt reactions to market moves, but it also assumes that the markets are liquid. Most of UBS's equity derivatives related to Asian stockmarkets. In 1997 there was a financial crisis in Asia, during which currencies and stockmarkets crashed. Union Bank's dynamic hedging understandably went haywire – futures prices and the underlying equity prices lost their usually close relationship. Further losses were incurred because an incoming Labour government in Britain changed the law on the taxation of stock dividends. There were more losses on a portfolio of Japanese equity warrants stripped from convertible bonds. The losses from these operations run by the near-autonomous global equity derivatives department of Ramy Goldstein, a former Israeli army officer, eventually reached Sfr1.5 billion ($1 billion). The fiasco turned merger discussions with rival Swiss Bank Corporation into more of a takeover.

The crash of world stockmarkets ten years earlier, in October 1987, should have been enough to warn traders of equity derivatives that markets can periodically become dysfunctional. When they do, the relationship between the equity market and the futures market breaks down, especially if, as in the case of various markets in 1987 and 1997, equity trading is halted for a day or so. In 1987, computerised trading rules, so-called program trading, appear to have exacerbated the problem: falling stock prices triggered automatic selling, which drove prices down further, triggering further selling in a vicious spiral.

Gambler's ruin

Derivatives are dangerous when exposure to them is in the hands of someone trading on conviction or intuition or, even worse, out of desperation, who loses track of the risks involved. Such emotive reasoning is usually wrong and expensive. Take the case of Nick Leeson at Baring Brothers, a British bank. His futures trades in the Japanese Nikkei stock index and Japanese government bond futures were initially based on the conviction that Japanese equities would bounce back. After the Kobe earthquake in January 1995 he doubled his bets on a recovery of the Nikkei index. The unfortunate property of derivatives is that losses can rapidly be compounded. Leeson lost about four times as much money for Barings between February 2nd and February 23rd, when he absconded from the bank, as he had before the Kobe earthquake.

Two other cases in the early 1990s showed how quickly and devastatingly non-financial companies could lose money in derivatives once they had loss-making positions that were well known in the market. Both were German, and both got out of their depth in oil futures contracts. Klöckner & Co, one of Europe's great privately owned oil-trading companies, put too much trust in Peter Henle, its finance director. Henle bet the ranch on oil futures, losing the company an estimated $380m by October 1988. Deutsche Bank stepped in, took over the positions and was able to sell them off gradually in the market. In December 1993 Metallgesellschaft, a German metal production and trading company, discovered huge losses in oil futures emanating from MGRM, its small trading operation in Baltimore, Maryland. Arthur Benson had been selling long-dated contracts that guaranteed to deliver heating oil and other petroleum products all over America at future dates. Benson was a firm believer in backwardation, a common phenomenon in commodity futures, in which the future price stays below the cost of buying oil today. It is possible to win by buying futures and watching their price rise towards maturity. Hedging itself in this way, MGRM sold heating-oil contracts to customers. Benson was prepared to bet on backwardation persisting over the next few years. Unfortunately it did not, and he was soon left facing contracts to deliver products at prices far higher than those he had reckoned with. As the oil traders got to know about Metallgesellschaft's big futures position they traded against it mercilessly, especially at the quarterly rollover dates of the Nymex oil futures market. Metallgesellschaft was trading on margin, as do all oil traders, and as its positions were increasingly lossmaking its counterparties demanded more and more collateral. Ultimately, Metallgesellschaft's bankers and accountants in Frankfurt were alerted to the problem and refused to put up more cash. Again, it was Deutsche Bank that stepped in to take over the positions and to trade out of them; the estimated losses were DM1.87 billion (see Chapter 14).

Putting off the evil day

The use of derivatives in each case both accelerated the losses and allowed those losses to be hidden from internal or external controllers. A derivative or futures contract usually concerns a promise to deliver something at some future date. The anticipated cost of that future obligation varies according to today's valuation. If that valuation can somehow be deferred or tampered with, then the future obligation may not look so devastating. Leeson fooled his masters at Barings about the true extent of the losses he had built up. For months, even years, he was able to roll over (postpone for another three months) the bank's obligation to pay for losses on Nikkei futures contracts. Like a large snowball, those losses increased each time they were rolled over.

In all the above cases, the derivatives contracts were written between professionals such as corporate treasurers or corporate dealers and banks or professional traders. Each side went into the contract with its eyes open – and in theory the speculation could have gone either way, depending on market movements.

In the mid-1990s, there was a spate of derivatives contracts that were different, in that they were designed to deceive. These were artifices such as quanto swaps and LIBOR squared (the London interbank offered rate – the interest rate at which London-based banks lend to each other – multiplied by itself), which exposed their buyers to losses that bore no relation to any positions that they might have wanted to hedge.

Take the quanto swap. The essence of an interest-rate or currency swap is that it separates a notional principal amount from the flow of interest payments. Swaps were originally designed with a notional principal amount in mind, such as the proceeds of a bond issue. The interest payments related to that bond issue were swapped with the interest payments on a floating-rate loan of the same notional amount. The swap switched the swapper's exposure from fixed rate to floating rate or vice versa. This could be useful in the case of, say, a mortgage lender, lending fixed-rate mortgages to clients, who found it was cheaper to borrow at floating rate and do a swap into a fixed rate than to borrow fixed-rate funds directly.

Similarly, with a currency swap, one party would borrow in a currency in which it could borrow cheapest, then swap the proceeds and the interest payments with a borrower who could borrow more cheaply in another currency. Each party used the other as a source of cheaper funds.

Losing touch with reality

Rather like a cubist painting, the quanto swap deliberately jumbled up the elements of interest-rate and currency swaps. A quanto swapper could choose to make interest payments at an interest rate indexed to that of another currency. So, for example, you could choose to pay interest on a notional loan of Japanese yen over five years in dollars, at floating-rate yen interest rates. You are simply taking a bet that your dollar repayments will be lower, either because of lower yen interest rates, or because the dollar loses value against the yen. You can either win or lose on this bet, but it bears no relation to any underlying economic liability that you might have.

Swap flows based on highly geared gambles on interest rates were equally perverse. Swap clients were often persuaded, particularly when an interest-rate trend seemed firmly set in, to be party to instruments that exposed them to extreme losses if the market turned against them. They were paid handsomely over prevailing interest rates to take the exposure, and they had an ill-founded conviction that the market would not turn. Just as the finance director of Hammersmith & Fulham was sure that sterling interest rates would continue to fall in 1988, so many treasurers around the world were convinced that dollar interest rates in 1994 would fall rather than rise.

LIBOR squared was the most pernicious. Counterparties accepted a cash flow at a high fixed rate of interest in return for an obligation to pay the square of the dollar LIBOR interest rate. This was fine when, for example, the fixed-rate income flow was 12% and LIBOR was at 3%. But a simple one percentage point rise in LIBOR would lift the floating-rate payment to 16%. No treasurer in his right mind would have entered such a contract if he had had the remotest suspicion that interest rates would rise that far, rather than fall. Unfortunately, the chairman of the US Federal Reserve confounded them all, and many investment bankers too, with a sudden hike of short-term rates in February 1994, from 3% to 3.25%: enough to throw many leveraged interest-rate bets into confusion and sudden loss.

Oranges and lemons

One of the losers was Orange County Investment Pool in California. The county treasurer had enjoyed success during the years of declining interest rates before 1994. Encouraged by his advisers, Merrill Lynch, he made leveraged bets on the differential between long-term and short-term rates, pledging his investments as collateral in order to make more bets. Some of those bets involved structured notes that earned well while rates held but would lose heavily if short-term rates rose. Some bets were on the differential between German and American interest rates. Orange County's $7.5 billion in funds became a leveraged portfolio with $20.5 billion of exposure to a rise in interest rates. As rates began to rise in 1994, Merrill Lynch offered to close out Orange County's positions, but the treasurer, convinced that rates would fall again, hung on. The final loss was $1.6 billion, bankrupting the county.

Another loser was Gibson Greetings, which had signed several contracts with Bankers Trust that lost it $23m after the 1994 interest-rate rises. They included a LIBOR squared contract in which Gibson received a fixed rate from Bankers Trust and paid out the square of the dollar LIBOR rate in return, which was fine until rates started rising. Procter & Gamble, a detergent maker, also wrote several contracts with Bankers Trust that began to lose heavily when interest rates rose. In one case it ended up paying Bankers Trust over 14% above the normal commercial paper rate. In another it lost a bet that D-mark interest rates would stay within a set range and ended up paying Bankers Trust 16%. Procter & Gamble sued Bankers Trust for selling it "inappropriate" derivatives; it got $150m to help cover its $195m of losses.

Many investment banks had been selling such products. There were some celebrated cases in East Asia, in which counterparties either would not or could not pay up.

It was a turning point for sellers of derivatives. After about 15 years of fantastic growth in their use, this season of losses made the sellers and their customers far more aware of the products' hidden potential as an accelerator of losses. From now on more attention was paid to the "appropriateness" of derivatives sold: customers must understand how the product they are buying might perform in adverse conditions. For non-professional customers, and even for smaller, less sophisticated companies, the onus was on derivative sellers to explain the dynamics of what they were selling.

Long-term repercussions

But even professionals can get the dynamics wrong, as has been seen time and again. Perhaps the classic case was that of Long-Term Capital Management (LTCM), a hedge fund that blew up spectacularly in 1998. LTCM's reason for existence was its alleged ability to quantify the relative risks in the market and judge the dynamics of, for example, one government bond price against another. LTCM exposed itself to the performance of billions of dollars worth of government bonds, which its own quantitative analysis showed were certain to converge in price – it was only a question of time. Because the LTCM experts were so sure they were right they leveraged their bet, doubling and redoubling their positions by means of interest-rate swaps, and waited.

Unfortunately, these bets coincided with a crisis in Asia and then one in Russia. All government bond prices were affected, even American Treasury bonds. Worse than the price, trading in all but a few bonds became illiquid, which meant that buying and selling bonds to adjust LTCM's position became either impossible or hopelessly expensive. What is more, because LTCM's positions were so big, other players in the market knew them, or guessed them, and raised their prices when LTCM traders called. It was a disaster for LTCM. Its counterparties, knowing of LTCM's lossmaking positions, asked it for collateral to cover the exposure. LTCM had to sell its winning positions to raise the collateral. It was losing money and no longer had the resources to ride out the storm. When 14 banks took over its positions, they had the capital to ride the storm and finally, a year later, reap the rewards of LTCM's analysis. LTCM's long-term prediction of how bond prices would move was correct, but it ran out of the time and money needed for its positions to come right.

Again, this was an important, and spectacular, lesson on how big bets in derivatives and/or leveraged positions (not necessarily using derivatives) can be intellectually right but still go horribly wrong (see Chapter 15).

As a reminder that derivatives, badly managed, can still accelerate deadly losses, there was the case of Allied Irish Banks (AIB) in March 2002. John Rusnak, a foreign-exchange trader in the Baltimore office of Allfirst, an AIB subsidiary, with the use of foreign-exchange options and futures, was able to roll over foreign-exchange losses, which totalled $631m by the time they were discovered and halted. Like Nick Leeson, Rusnak had been able to reassure his risk controllers that the positions mostly cancelled each other out, so that the bank's net exposure was low. In fact the net lossmaking positions were huge. Without the use of options and futures to roll over losses and double his bets, Rusnak's losses would have been more limited.

Don't let anyone get away with telling you that derivatives are not dangerous. Like driving at high speed, they require extra understanding and vigilance and better hardware and software. A risk manager who is not aware of the danger and of the uncanny ability of his fellow humans to mess things up is not a good risk manager.

4 Temples to risk management

Charles Sanford probably counts as one of the great visionaries of modern risk management, although that vision did not save his firm from embarking on a voyage of self-destruction. He was chairman of Bankers Trust from 1987 to 1995. Bankers Trust Company of New York was a banker's bank: it had only large clients, mostly other banks. Sanford decided in the early 1980s that making large loans to companies and sovereign borrowers was a mug's game. The profit margin was small yet the consequences of one company or one country not repaying its loans were huge, in terms of management time and loan loss provisions. A bank like Bankers Trust, he concluded, could make more profit from arranging loans and other financial services for clients, and then passing the risk on to other risktakers, such as pension funds, cash-rich companies, or other, less agile banks. Under Sanford's chairmanship Bankers Trust transformed itself from being purely a lending bank into one that bought and sold derivatives, arranged complex financial transactions and made markets in exotic financial instruments, at the same time making sure that it ended up holding little of the financial risk itself.

Twenty-twenty vision

In August 1993 Sanford spelled out his vision in a speech, "Financial Markets in 2020". He foresaw a world in which every form of financial risk could be identified, quantified, split up and sold to the buyer with the most appropriate appetite. The quantification had become possible because of the rapid development of computer power. He anticipated personal "wealth accounts", which would be invested in a plethora of the most suitable financial assets. The wealth account would be so flexible and marketable that "wealth cards" would "allow you to pay for your sports car by instantly drawing on part of the wealth inherent in your vacation house". In effect, individuals would have the option to manage their own mutual fund. Financial firms, such as Bankers Trust, would be selling to "market segments of one".

Sanford believed in a concept that he called "particle finance". It was a highly optimistic attempt to analyse risk down to its smallest particle, so that, in the end, little would be left to chance. Human nature was always prone to fads and irrational exuberance, but by 2020 much more about markets would be understood and harnessed appropriately.

He philosophised as follows:

> *As risk management becomes ever more precise and customised, the amount of risk that we all have to bear will be greatly reduced, lowering the need for financial capital. This will have a tremendous social value because financial capital that had been required to cushion these risks will be available elsewhere in society to produce more wealth to address society's needs. In addition, this will liberate human capital by the greater leveraging of talent.*

He predicted in 1993 that financial risk management would move towards a finer analysis of credit risk and the increasing tradability of financial exposures.

But he never claimed that computer power and particle finance would plug all the gaps: "The ideal of a perfectly efficient market will not be achieved by 2020, if ever." This is just as well for his own intellectual reputation, because, like all human endeavours before or since, Sanford's long-term theorising blinded him to the closer realities that financial dealers face every day: deception, dishonesty, market manipulation and fraud. These realities and his neglect of them sank his own firm.

But that does not invalidate the noble efforts of Bankers Trust under Sanford to become less a bank and more an academy of risk management. Bankers Trust coined the term Raroc – risk-adjusted return on capital – an attempt to quantify risk in terms of the anticipated or actual return on capital that is achieved by taking that risk. For example, an activity such as selling equity options might achieve high returns in terms of option premiums, but the risk of sudden big losses is also high. Therefore the capital needed to cushion a sudden big loss should be more for this activity than for, say, handling money transfers. Both are banking activities. One brings in considerably more revenue than the other, most of the time. But returns on the first are more volatile than those on the second.

Bankers Trust attempted to apply Raroc to its entire spectrum of businesses, and to reward its employees on the basis of capital they used and the returns that the allocated capital produced. Now risk-based capital allocation has become common practice among financial firms, although it is generally acknowledged that the allocation of capital is more of an applied art than an exact science.

Banking used to be a simple activity. A bank took deposits and made loans, taking basically two risks: that a borrower would fail to repay, and that depositors would suddenly demand to withdraw their money. A bank made its money by lending at a higher rate and for a longer term than it borrowed from its depositors. The risks were simple but stark. The default of a big borrower could lead to a run on the bank and, possibly, the demise of the bank or its takeover by another bank or government intervention.

Multiplying complexity

Nowadays the biggest banks have become far more complex, often including insurance, investment banking and asset management, as well as lending and trading activities. In theory, the complexity has the effect of spreading the risks over many businesses and reduces the chance that one stark event will lead to the failure of the bank. But in fact complexity adds new dimensions of risk. If these new risks are not identified and continuously monitored, they can also be damaging to a bank, though perhaps not fatal. The attempt to monitor and manage risks centrally over the entire range of a bank's businesses – firm-wide risk management, as it is called – became a much-touted activity in the 1990s (see Chapter 7). In the early 1990s, Bankers Trust began to compile a database of operational risks: the sort of losses that are caused not by market or credit events but by other factors, such as bureaucratic mistakes, computer failure, fires, blackouts or the loss of documents. It was an attempt to factor in every possible threat to the firm's continuity. It is clear, however, that the low-cost, more frequent occurrences, such as documentary errors and small systems failures, are easier to quantify and factor in than the really big shocks, such as fraud by a rogue trader or a terrorist attack (see Chapter 8).

Besides Bankers Trust, another big American bank, J.P. Morgan & Co, was an early pioneer of firm-wide risk management. Dennis Weatherstone, chairman until December 1994, used to demand a report at 4.15pm each day (called the 4.15 report), giving a snapshot of the firm's risk positions worldwide and what might happen to them over the next 24 hours.

J.P. Morgan took over the mantle of Bankers Trust as an academy of risk. It spent a lot of effort analysing correlation: the extent to which an event or price change in one market affects other markets and prices around the world. Correlation is the opposite of diversification. If an investment portfolio is spread across various markets that do not affect each other the correlation is low, and the portfolio has a better chance of maintaining its overall value when one market drops. J.P. Morgan developed a database known as RiskMetrics, which offered users a common basis for calculations of the volatility and correlation of various financial markets and financial instruments around the world. In 1994 it made RiskMetrics freely available on the internet.

RiskMetrics was supposed to be cutting-edge financial technology, but the fact that it was given away free suggested that it was already past its usefulness to J.P. Morgan. RiskMetrics was based on the concept of value-at-risk (VaR). The volatility and correlation matrix showed you what your biggest expected loss (VaR) would be over a given period. But only up to a point: the VaR calculation did not take into account extreme market conditions, when correlation and volatility go off the scale. And it never claimed to, since it always reckoned to be wrong for a percentage of the time, usually between one and five days out of every 100.

Despite this blind spot, VaR is useful for making trading decisions and for dealing in relatively calm markets (see Chapter 5). The temptation, however, is to use it to judge the overall risk of market losses that a firm is exposed to, because it produces a convenient finite number for maximum expected loss.

Bond value shock

In February 1994 Alan Greenspan, chairman of the US Federal Reserve, raised dollar interest rates a quarter of a percentage point and continued to raise them through the spring. The effect of this easily foreseeable decision on the price of American Treasury bonds and other medium-term dollar instruments was more traumatic than any VaR model had anticipated. Bond dealers, even at the most astute financial firms such as Goldman Sachs, lost millions of dollars because of an exaggerated fall in the price of medium- and long-term bonds. It was a warning to the most sophisticated firms that they could at any time be exposed to sudden losses, even in apparently benign markets, from a sharp, unexpected and even irrational change in market prices. Firms such as J.P. Morgan and Goldman Sachs intensified their efforts to guard against sudden reversals.

To combat the scepticism of regulators, who feared that new financial techniques might endanger the stability of the system, there was an unprecedented sharing of information between financial firms, consultants and trade associations and publication of the results.

In 1993, the Group of Thirty, a body based in Washington and funded by the private sector (mostly banks), produced a detailed checklist of risk-management principles for banks and investment banks. The group's members are senior financial officials from the government and private sector. Its chairman until 2001 was Paul Volcker, former chairman of the US Federal Reserve. The 1993 checklist was developed by the G30's derivatives study group, which was drawn entirely from banks active in the derivatives sector.

In 1997, Coopers & Lybrand, an accounting and consulting firm (now part of PricewaterhouseCoopers), published a more compressed *Manual of Generally Accepted Risk Principles* (GARP). There were 89 of these, attempting to cover every possible eventuality that could affect a financial firm. The first 12 principles were about how to handle risk management at board level, by clearly defining responsibilities and establishing the independence of a risk control department, which is responsible for ensuring that checks and balances on the business are carried out and that procedures are properly complied with. The next section dealt with the function of risk management (not the same as risk control). Risk managers monitor and review exposure limits for each line of business and for the whole firm. There are 36 principles that deal with risk measurement and reporting, concentrating on producing numbers for value-at-risk.

In 1998, Goldman Sachs and Swiss Bank Corporation collaborated on a book, *The Practice of Risk Management*, which outlined their different approaches to firm-wide risk management. It included an account of "a day in the life of a risk manager". One increasingly important exercise for these firms was stress-testing: calculating the effect of extreme events on the health and wealth of a financial institution. This is done largely by imagining worst-case scenarios, such as the worst imaginable market shocks, a combination of, for example, the stockmarket crash of 1987, the European currency crisis of 1992 and the bond market crisis of 1994. Stress-testing tries to anticipate future shocks, rather than relying on a replay of historical events. However, it is limited by the risk-manager's ability to imagine what might happen. The way a financial crisis plays out is too complex to be mapped in advance by mathematics (see Chapter 13). But this has not discouraged scenario-planning and stress-testing.

Non-operating manual

The Practice of Risk Management was published in 1998. In August that year both Goldman and SBC Warburg were caught by the next crisis, when Russia decided to default on its dollar-denominated domestic debt. There was an unprecedented rush to the safety of the most liquid American Treasury bonds – any old American Treasury bond would not do. This precipitated the collapse of Long-Term Capital Management (LTCM), which for a time seemed to threaten the entire financial system (see Chapter 15). The chain of events showed that, however sophisticated risk-management practices had become, those who were supposedly at the forefront of identifying risks could still fail to sniff a crisis that was developing right under their noses.

This happened despite an unprecedented flourishing of risk-management consultancies and software companies. The modern, computer-aided risk-management industry grew up after the mid-1980s, alongside the phenomenal development of derivatives. Software companies rushed to provide automated systems that could help steer risk managers through the fast-moving complexities of highly geared financial positions. It was a competitive business, but as noted in Chapter 3, the wrong information or the wrong calculation could quickly lead to accelerated losses.

The new dimension added to risk management was the ability of the computer to go through many complex calculations in an increasingly short time. A basic technique is Monte Carlo simulation, the exploration of many possible outcomes. For example, instead of going through the laborious business of tossing a coin or spinning a roulette wheel thousands of times to establish the probability of each outcome, the computer can simulate the exercise. In the case of a market simulation, it can change variables for each separate series of calculations, changing the interest rate, the exchange rate, the relative prices of equities and bonds, and so on, in almost endless variation. A pattern of probabilities is established on which trading and hedging decisions can be made.

As the computer software for these calculations developed, it became increasingly user-friendly. So a risk manager could see graphically, in terms of peaks, troughs and colours, where exactly the area of hottest risk, or highest potential reward, would be found.

Victorian optimism

In the early 1990s there was a sense of excitement that all of this could be quantified and put to use by risk managers for the benefit of humanity. The risk-management community was like a mountaineering club. Individual traders and individual firms might make mistakes, but the safety equipment was improving all the time. There was faith that with well-maintained equipment and the right degree of circumspection, the mountain of risk run by complex financial firms could be mapped and conquered.

In parallel with the software companies, which broadly were encouraging the combination and mastery of ever more complex risks, were the doom-mongers. These were the voices of caution, continually warning that there was more risk out there than any of these financial firms bargained for. Among them were Henry Kaufman, former chief economist at Salomon Brothers; Charles Smithson, who worked at Chase Manhattan Bank before heading the CIBC (Canadian Imperial Bank of Commerce) School of Financial Products; and Leslie Rahl, formerly a derivatives manager at Citibank, who in 1994 set up Capital Market Risk Advisors in New York.

Smithson's CIBC school and Rahl's advisers appeared almost to exult in the blunders and miscalculations of the recent past. Each one provided a lesson for the future. The weakest link in modern risk management was "model risk", the tendency for a simplified view of the market to apparently work well for a while and then go horribly wrong.

False impressions

A good principle to bear in mind is that every model, whether it is an aspect of the financial market or anything else – a model steam engine or a hydroelectric dam – will behave differently from the real thing, especially in extreme conditions. A model that appears to replicate market behaviour perfectly in certain circumstances is likely to go off course if circumstances change too much. For example, a model that predicted a convergence in the prices of various American government bonds, whose prices had got out of line, no longer worked when Russia defaulted in 1998. This apparently unrelated event caused a rush to quality in Treasury bonds, driving the bond prices apart in defiance of mathematics and reason. This was a tremendous lesson for risk managers, but it did not come until August 1998, and it will not prevent them from making other false assumptions in future.

For several years in a row, Smithson's academy published an account of the biggest risk-management bungles. But when the CIBC school was closed in the late 1990s, Smithson set up his own advisory firm, Rutter Associates, specialising in credit and operational risk. Rahl's website (www.cmra.com) used to carry a running total of the major risk-management losses since the beginning of the 1990s. Now a similar Wheel of Misfortune can be found on the website of Erisk (erisk.com), which has also compiled a library of case studies on these foul-ups (see Figure 4.1).

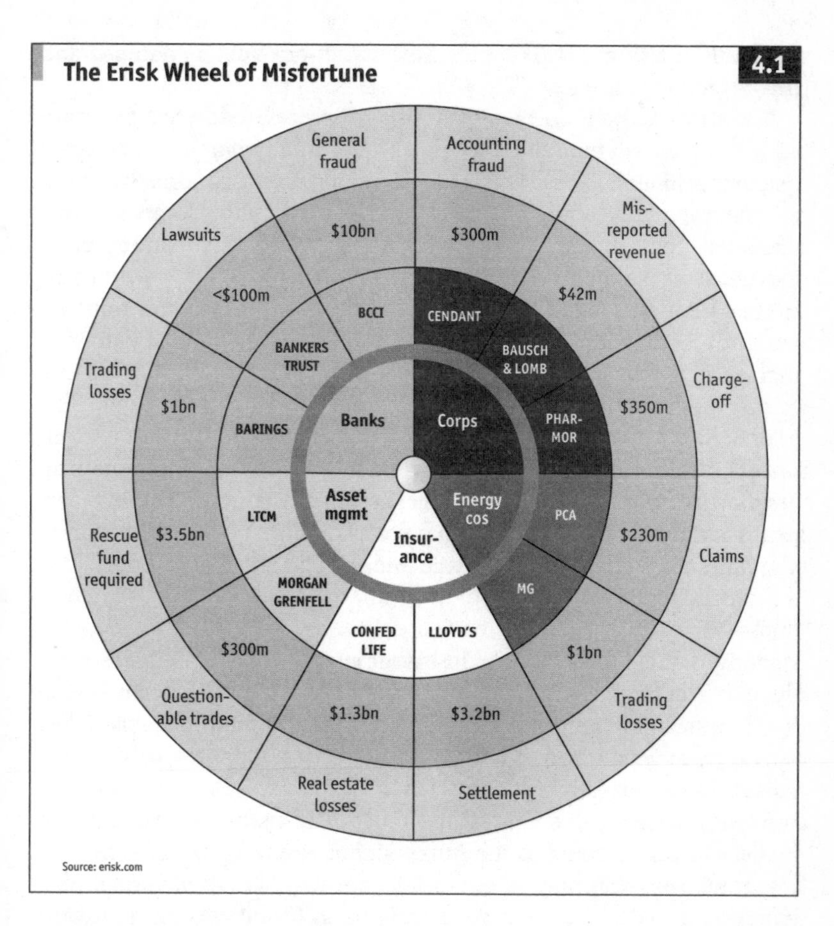

Maths versus psychology

The risk-management community can be divided roughly into those that expect models, and the best efforts of risk managers, to be fallible and to fail regularly, and those that prefer to see risk management as a scientific addition to the product range, as means to further enhancing financial returns. Both are valid approaches. The first is more a study of human nature and the second an applied science.

Many consultants and software firms have codified risk-management procedures into a range of standard or tailor-made commercial products. Algorithmics, a company run by Ron Denbo, is possibly the best at self-publicity. Algorithmics provides its clients, mainly investment banks, with a means of calculating their preferences for profit and loss:

assuming you are going to lose, how much are you prepared to lose before "regret" outweighs the willingness to gamble?

Consultants such as PricewaterhouseCoopers, Ernst & Young and Mercer Oliver Wyman have advised banks on a firm-wide approach to risk management. Each one has its risk-management lexicon, like GARP. Consultants are also hired by banks, or by financial regulators, to investigate accidents when a financial scandal breaks. Sometimes special panels are set up to investigate the chain of events in the wake of such crises as Barings, Metallgesellschaft or LTCM. All these have added to the body of wisdom (after the event), making it theoretically possible that no egregious financial blunder will be repeated.

Just to show that this is not always the case, in March 2002 Allied Irish Banks (AIB) obliged with almost a carbon copy of the Barings crisis of 1995. A trusted trader at a small subsidiary of Barings, remote from head office, was apparently making consistently good profits with low-risk derivatives business. Even though his trading volumes were huge, any questions from headquarters were met with reassurances from local management that everything was under control. When alarm bells finally rang it was too late; the trader had been doubling his bets and cleverly hiding losses. Barings lost around £850m and collapsed. AIB, a much bigger bank, lost only $691m. But that was eight years later, when the lesson about controls over remote outposts should have been thoroughly drummed into any half-sophisticated international bank. It happened again in January 2004 when National Australia Bank, the country's biggest bank, confessed that four of its traders had built up losses in foreign-exchange options totalling anything from A$185m to A$600m. They had apparently been operating as an exclusive team, better paid and aloof from the bank's main foreign-exchange traders. Elementary rules of risk management had been ignored.

A growing religion

The culture of risk management has reinforced itself by making much of such shocks, analysing them on websites and picking over them in academic papers. Informal groups have grown up, such as the Global Association of Risk Professionals (confusingly also known as GARP) and the International Association of Financial Engineers (IAFE). There are annual round tables, such as the International Finance and Commodities Institute (IFCI), now known as the International Financial Risk Institute (www.riskinstitute.ch), and online journals, such as erisk.com, netexposure.com and numa.com. Various magazines also specialise in risk management: *Risk*, *Derivatives Week* and *FOW*. The message conveyed by most of these sources is that derivatives and other leveraged products have been unfairly maligned. If their risks are understood, they can be useful tools. The implication is that the people behind the words you are reading – the coterie of risk-management professionals – know better. They have seen the pitfalls and so there is steady progress towards a better understanding of the way financial markets and institutions behave. With this new wisdom it is possible to make more money or to lose less. The bad news is that even the risk-management professionals can mess things up, and they frequently do. One message of this book is that humans' attempts to predict and master what is in effect their own collective behaviour have always and will constantly fall short of reality. This is equally true whether it is the behaviour of societies, football teams, investment banks or financial markets. Financial markets are particularly rich territory in this respect because they almost instantly reflect each new piece of information or disinformation. They are a game, yet at the same time they affect the fortunes of individuals, of companies and of countries.

Charles Sanford was a visionary, but at the same time he was too optimistic about human behaviour and the ability of man and machine to identify and sell every separate particle of risk.

5 Models for Everyman

Backtrack a bit to 1996. There is a collision of two forces. On one side, bank regulators are increasingly worried that banks have learned to sidestep their prudential rules; on the other side, the banks, anticipating tougher regulation, are determined to have a say in how that regulation is shaped. Financial markets and the management of banking risk have become so complex that they are only properly understood by the banks themselves. Regulators, rating agencies, securities analysts and all other experts that could exercise appropriate checks and balances on banks have been left floundering. If you do not understand the dynamics of zero-coupon yield curves, binomial trees and volatility smiles, you are not versed in the language of risk management. That was the prevailing climate. Regulators, somewhat blinded by science, were reaching the conclusion that they must learn to understand and then speak the same language.

This was possibly their biggest mistake. But it began there, in 1996. It concerned the way regulators set banks' regulatory capital: that is, the minimum amount of capital that banks should carry, given the size and riskiness of their assets.

A commonsense cushion

A rule of thumb has generally been 8%: if a bank has made $100m of loans, it needs $8m of capital to cushion it against the failure of some borrowers to repay. In the 18th and 19th centuries banks usually had a much higher percentage of capital to risk assets, between 25% and 40%. But that was at a time when it was perhaps more difficult to enforce credit checks, bankruptcy procedures and suchlike. In some less developed countries, even today, prudent banks may carry that proportion of capital. But in western economies in the 1980s, regulators considered 8% a fair level for banks that operated and competed internationally.

Of course not all bank assets involve the same risk. A loan to a bank's home government, for example, is safer than the bank itself. Regulators at that time agreed that the credit risk on such loans was so low that it would require no capital backing at all. The regulators, in this case, were an informal group of central bankers from the world's top ten industrial countries who met regularly at the Bank for International Settlements (BIS) in Basel, Switzerland. The group became known as the Basel Committee on Banking Supervision, or the Cooke Committee, after its first chairman, Peter Cooke of the Bank of England. (Note that until 2000 the anglicised spelling Basle was used. At that late date, central bankers noticed that Basel was the spelling used locally in this German-speaking part of Switzerland.)

In the early 1980s, the Basel committee began to work on a list of credit weightings for different classes of assets: zero for the government debt of industrial countries (members of the Organisation for Economic Co-operation and Development – OECD); 20% for loans to OECD-based banks; and 100% for loans to non-bank companies. Very simply, this meant that a $100m loan to a non-bank company would require $8m of capital, a $100m loan to an OECD-based bank would require $1.6m (20% of $8m), and a loan to an OECD government would require zero capital. The committee also for the first time included so-called off-balance-sheet credit risks. These are credit exposures that result from contracts such as interest-rate and currency swaps, options and forward foreign-exchange contracts.

Credit risk in an interest-rate swap

A $100m interest-rate swap does not carry as much credit risk as a $100m loan. The reason is that the principal sum underlying the swap is not at risk, because it is only a notional amount. The important exposure in a swap is the risk that one counterparty or the other, at one payment date, will fail to pay the net difference between the floating interest rate and the agreed fixed interest rate. For example, imagine that a bank (Ziggurat Bank) and a company (Agora) have agreed a five-year $100m interest-rate swap. Ziggurat has promised to pay Agora the prevailing floating rate each year, plus 2%; Agora has promised to pay Ziggurat 6% fixed. At the end of year one the floating interest rate is 5%. According to their bargain, Ziggurat should pay Agora $7m (5% plus 2%) of the notional $100m – remember neither party has lent the other any money, they have just agreed to swap cash flows – and Agora should pay Ziggurat $6m. On a net basis Ziggurat simply pays Agora the difference between the $7m and the $6m, which is $1m. Easy.

At the end of year two, the floating rate is 4%. Ziggurat and Agora each owe the other $6m, so they are quits and no payment is made. At the end of year three, the floating rate has dropped to 2%. Ziggurat owes $4m (2% plus 2%) and Agora owes $6m – the difference due from Agora is $2m. Unfortunately, on the eve of making this payment Agora goes bust. Ziggurat is owed an immediate payment of $2m. Moreover, since

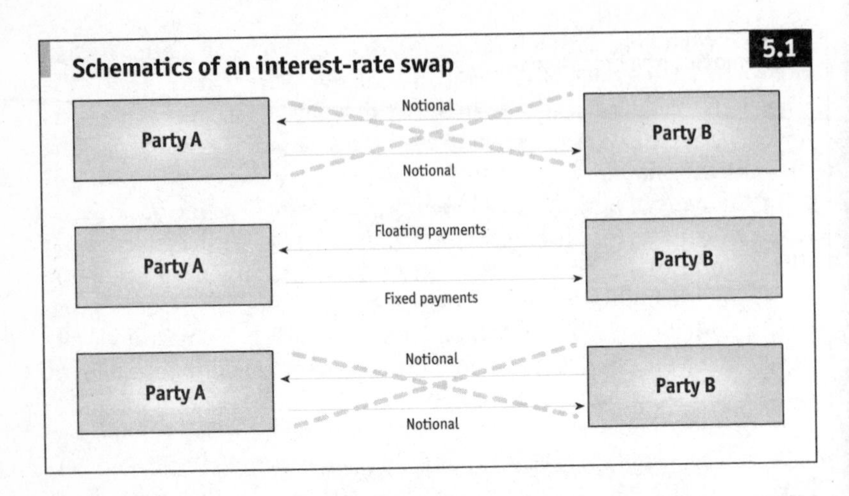

Agora has now gone bust, it will not be there as a counterparty at the end of years four and five. The net payments at those dates are also likely to have been in Ziggurat's favour – possibly $3.5m for year four and $4.5m for year five – as interest rates have been on a downward trend. So the termination of the swap has cost Ziggurat more than the $2m. By the end of year five it could have lost around $10m on the swap.

This is certainly nowhere near the full notional amount of the swap, $100m, but it is not a negligible loss. Nor is it an easy calculation. After all, nobody knows where interest rates will be at the end of years four and five; they can only make an intelligent guess.

The risk of loss from counterparty failure on a swap can only be guessed at, not known. The size of the possible loss is a function of how many years the swap has to run and the degree of uncertainty about interest rates, often referred to as volatility.

Credit risk in a currency swap

The Basel regulators developed a simple formula to calculate the potential credit exposure on an interest-rate swap, which depends on the time-span of the swap and the creditworthiness of the counterparty. They set the credit risk at 1% for every year the swap has to run, and applied the credit weighting on that 1% in the same way as they did for loans, then knocked off 50% in recognition that swap counterparties are usually more creditworthy than most – a rash assumption, as it turned out.

So the regulatory capital needed for a five-year $100m interest-rate

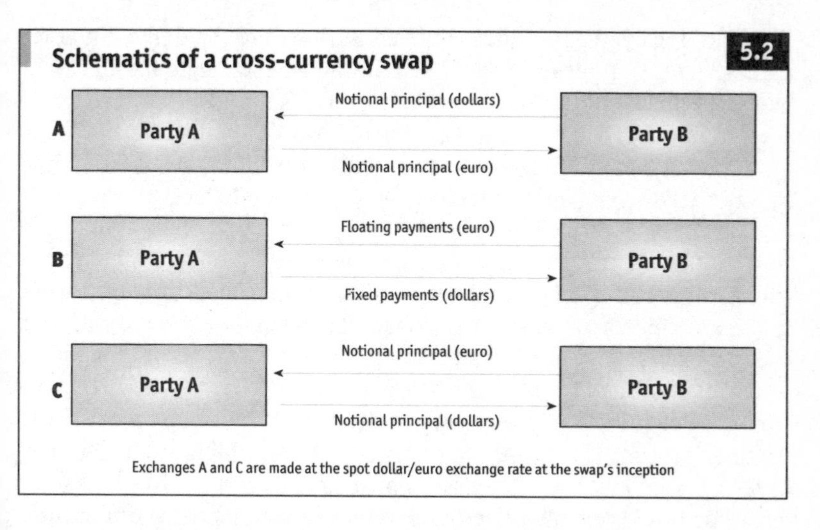

swap with a company such as Agora would have been 8% of five times $1m (that is, 8% of 1% of $100m each year times five), which is $400,000, with 50% off for extra creditworthiness, which is $200,000.

This is not a huge amount of capital for contracts that can quickly build up in one side's favour, leaving a considerable credit exposure. The more a counterparty sees a swap move in its favour, the more cautious it should be about the other side's creditworthiness, just as a gambler, the more he wins, is more anxious about the loser's ability to pay up. In most cases, these days, a counterparty will ask for collateral, such as cash or bonds, to cover the amount that the other party owes (or is likely to owe at the next payment date) on the swap.

Ziggurat Bank should have started asking Agora for collateral as soon as interest rates moved in its favour. If it had asked for, say, $6m of collateral some time in year three, even when Agora went bust it would have had $6m of its potential claim of $10m already in its possession.

The Basel regulators recognised that somewhat higher capital limits were required for swaps that involved an exchange-rate risk. These are so-called interest-rate and currency swaps, whereby one party notionally, or actually, borrows in, say, dollars and exchanges that obligation with another party which has notionally, or actually, borrowed the same principal amount in, say, yen. The two parties agree to service each other's debt, including an exchange of the borrowed amount at the end of the deal. For example, Ziggurat borrows $100m at 6% and Agora borrows ¥12 billion at a floating rate, which happens to be 1.5%. Both loans are for five years and, as the yen is at ¥120 to the dollar, the principal amounts are exactly equivalent at the outset. Ziggurat and Agora exchange their obligations. Ziggurat gets the yen and promises to pay the yen interest for five years; Agora gets the dollars and will pay the 6% annually on behalf of Ziggurat. At the end of the five years, Ziggurat has to pay back the yen and Agora must pay back the dollars.

Everything goes well until year three is nearly up, when Agora goes bust. At this point Agora owes Ziggurat an interest payment of $6m, but this is offset by the fact that the yen has appreciated to ¥100 to the dollar and interest rates are at 2%. Ziggurat owes Agora ¥240m, which at today's exchange rate is $2.4m. So Agora owes Ziggurat a net $3.6m when it goes bust. In most cases, where actual loans are involved, an exchange of principal is necessary at the end of the swap. Agora owes Ziggurat $100m. The dollar equivalent of the ¥12 billion that Ziggurat owes Agora is $120m at today's exchange rate. Ziggurat must pay Agora, or in this case Agora's liquidators, $20m less the net interest differential of $3.6m: a cool $16.4m. Even this crude example shows that a combined interest-rate and currency swap is a lot riskier than a simple interest-rate swap. The value-at-risk (VAR – a much-used term in this business) can be close to the full principal amount, and even more with highly volatile moves in interest rates and exchange rates over the several years of the swap.

Regulators accordingly applied a much tougher formula to the currency swap. The first year of the swap carried a 2% capital charge and each subsequent year another 3%. So in the case of the currency swap with Agora, Ziggurat would face a charge of 50% of 14% (2% plus four times 3%) of $100m: $7m. This is nearly as much as if Ziggurat had lent Agora the money. Even then, it did not cover Ziggurat's loss when Agora went bust, but it did mitigate it.

Jamming on the brakes

Before the regulators introduced these simple formulae in 1988, banks had been entering swap transactions without much heed to the credit risk. The 1988 Basel Accord put quite a brake on the currency swap market as banks applied a more realistic credit analysis.

The Basel Accord (known as Basel 1) was the bank regulators' first stab at using a quantitative approach to setting capital standards. In some ways it was taking a leaf out of the securities regulators' book. The Securities and Exchange Commission (SEC) in America had long applied "haircuts", or capital charges, to the big, temporary positions in shares or bonds that broker/dealers would hold when they were engaged in an underwriting.

The SEC's attitude to swaps, when they became common in the mid-1980s, was less sympathetic than that of its banking colleagues. It demanded that broker/dealers treat the credit exposure on a swap as if they were lending the whole notional amount: that is, $8m on $100m. It meant that broker/dealers could not act as principals in swaps, although they got around this constraint by booking the swaps with a related entity, such as a holding company or a separately capitalised subsidiary.

The SEC's attitude may ultimately have been the more sensible. With Basel 1, bank regulators set off on a stony path, attempting to write rules that kept abreast of new developments and products in an increasingly complex financial landscape. But if Basel 1 was a fork in the road, then an amendment to it, added in 1996, was the slippery slope.

The amendment had to do with market risk. Basel 1, for all its attempts at sophistication, left out a vital element of the risks that banks face: the sensitivity in the value of their assets to changes in market prices. For example, the value of a portfolio of medium-term bonds can be hit badly by a rise in interest rates. The value of assets denominated in foreign currencies, however stable their price in that currency, can yo-yo up and down on a bank's balance sheet as exchange rates fluctuate. Equity securities, or floating-rate bonds, are constantly subject to change.

Once the Basel committee established the principle that banks should carry capital according to the risk-weighted size, not the nominal size, of their assets, then the quest was on to find an ever more accurate measure of that riskiness. Basel 1 used crude formulas for the credit-equivalent risk of swaps, options and forward contracts. The 1996 amendment tried to apply more sophisticated formulas for setting market risk.

Into the lions' den

The investment banks and would-be investment banks were actively lobbying for regulators to see risk as they saw it, and to adjust their capital measures accordingly. The logic is compelling. If banks are taking risks, and are not hell-bent on their own destruction, then surely they will be applying the best and most sophisticated measures of prudence that they know. State-of-the-art risk management should also be the starting-point of state-of-the-art prudential regulation.

If only that were so. Unfortunately it is not. The psychology and incentives associated with running businesses at investment banks now enter the picture. There is what is called an agency problem. For example, Hank, a whizz-kid investment banker, trades a hot financial product, such as equity index options. He can sell options into the market which oblige his bank to pay out if the Dow Jones Industrial Average, or some other index, falls above or below a certain level. According to the level and the exercise price of the option, the bank is in danger of losing large amounts of money. The longer the term of the option, the more dangerous the position is.

To cover this danger, Hank has charged a premium for the options. The premium is calculated taking into account the past volatility of the index, and a guess at how much that volatility might increase during the life of the option. The money is taken immediately and looks good on Hank's profit-and-loss account. A prudent banker would put aside most or all of that money to cover eventualities, and perhaps to hedge part of the position, until all those options have expired. But calculating how much to put aside can be extremely difficult. If there is an actively traded market for the options then it is possible to calculate the cost of hedging, or of selling the whole position. But if the market is illiquid and few deals are done, there are few people expert enough to price the position apart from Hank himself and a handful of other traders at other firms.

Hank may be overoptimistic and underestimate the danger of his, or rather the bank's, position; in fact, he is almost bound to do so. The bank itself may be overoptimistic, relying too much on its sophisticated mathematical modelling, especially if it produces a healthy number on the bottom line. The attraction for Hank is that he will get a nice share of the profit reflected in his bonus, if his bets win. If his bets lose, he may forfeit his bonus, but he still gets his salary. The worst case is that he is fired. In the 1990s Hank would have had no trouble getting a job at another bank.

Pushing the envelope

The upshot of the agency problem is that investment banks, egged on by employees like Hank, have erred on the side of imprudence, especially in the case of long-dated derivative products with a limited trading history. Their mathematical models have been designed to guide them in a competitive market and to help them sail as close to the wind as possible.

It was a big step for Basel regulators to start flirting with the investment banks' own mathematical models, and to think of using them as a basis for setting levels of prudential capital.

But the banks' market risk management products in the mid-1990s looked good. Some of them started publishing figures for their everyday VAR. A lot of this activity was triggered by the losses many of them incurred in February 1994, when the US Federal Reserve Board unexpectedly raised interest rates several times. The rate hikes had a severe effect on the price of medium- and long-term bonds. Many traders and their risk managers, who should have known better, were caught out.

After that, these firms made a virtue of calculating every day what their maximum loss could be, given an extreme and unexpected change in market conditions: currency turmoil, a dramatic shift in interest rates, a stockmarket crash, or rocketing commodity prices. The VAR figure was reached by reckoning how much each portfolio of risks could lose in adverse conditions. The overall disastrous figure was reduced by assumptions that positions could be closed or hedged within, say, ten days, and that losses in some areas, such as currencies, would probably be offset by gains in interest rates, or vice versa. VAR was generally calculated within a 95–99% level of comfort. A 99% comfort level meant that losses might go above the VAR figure one day out of every 100. A 95% comfort level meant that VAR could be exceeded once every 20 days.

It is clear from this that VAR is a useful trading tool and that sudden increases in VAR can warn traders to reduce or hedge their positions. But it is also clear that VAR is a dangerous measure on which to bet the entire bank. If you did, the bank would have a probability of going bust one day in 100, or even one day in 20.

Nevertheless, in the mid-1990s regulators liked what banks were doing to identify their risks more closely. J.P. Morgan and Swiss Bank Corporation even published graphs in their annual reports, showing how their VAR – or in J.P. Morgan's case DEAR (daily earnings at risk) – had fared through the past year. The graphs handily showed how many days out of the year's 300 the loss had exceeded the VAR threshold (see Figure 5.3, which shows the VAR record of UBS Investment Bank in 2003).

These losses are not actual losses; they merely show how much the VAR of the bank's portfolio has moved when measured against the market. The valuation assumes that there would be a cost to closing the positions by selling them or hedging them.

Risks that offset each other

The clever trick in VAR is the estimate of correlation. Correlation is good or bad, depending on whether you are trying to find assets which

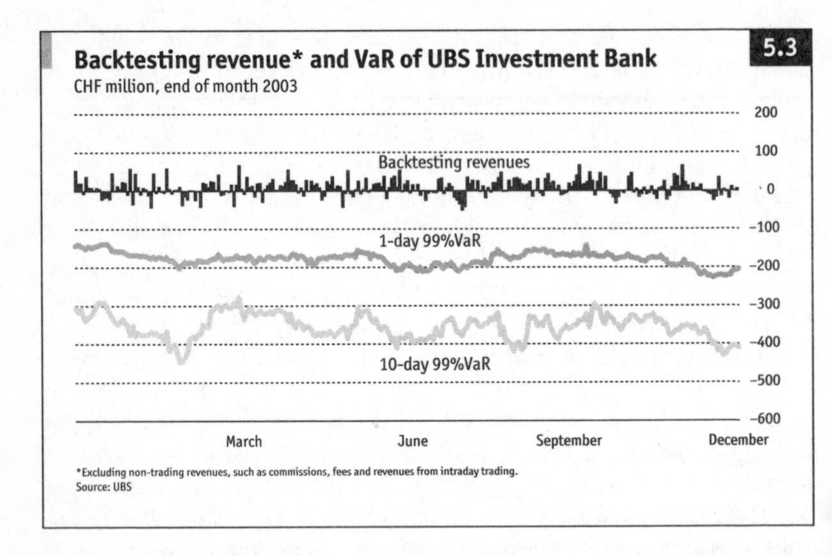

behave similarly in different market conditions, or which market conditions rarely affect in the same way. For example, if you are trying to hedge an asset, you would like the hedge to behave as nearly as possible like the asset itself. To hedge the risk of owning a government bond, the best proximate solution is to sell a bond future which has a close correlation with the bond itself: the price of the bond and the price of the future move more or less in step (or at least that is the theory). The closer this is to happening, the nearer the correlation between them moves towards the perfect 1.0 (the scale moves from 1.0, perfect correlation, to zero, where there is no correlation at all). The more diversified a portfolio of assets is, the lower in theory their correlation number is.

For estimating the VAR of a portfolio, it is clear that the more diversified the assets, the less correlated they are, and the less will be the overall impact of extreme market conditions. So VAR thrives on low correlations for diversified assets and high correlations for assets that are meant to hedge each other.

It is no surprise that investment banks have spent a great deal of energy studying the correlation, or lack of it, between different types of assets. How correlated, for example, are the interest rates of the dollar and sterling, the US dollar and the Hong Kong dollar, the Thai baht and the Malaysian ringgit? How correlated are American government bonds with corporate bonds? What are the correlations between oil, gold and platinum?

Table 5.1 **Correlation matrix,[a] 1994–2001**

	ELMI+	*ASIA*	*EUR*	*LATAM*	*SP500*	*EMFREE*	*EMBI+*	*GBI*	*MSHY*
ELMI+	1								
ASIA	0.95	1							
EUR	0.32	0.19	1						
LATAM	0.16	−0.02	−0.35	1					
SP500	0.27	0.1	0.21	0.18	1				
EMFREE	0.33	0.21	0.15	0.18	0.18	1			
EMBI+	−0.02	−0.3	0.34	0.65	0.34	0.43	1		
GBI	−0.01	−0.13	0.21	0.34	0.46	−0.4	0.36	1	
MSHY	−0.09	−0.28	0.45	0.26	0.67	0.05	0.57	0.73	1

a Correlation of various asset classes. 1= perfect correlation.

Notes:

ELMI+ J.P. Morgan regional family of indexes
ASIA Asian sub-index of the ELMI+
EUR European sub-index of the ELMI+
LATAM Latin America sub-index of the ELMI+
SP500 Standard & Poor's 500 index
EMFREE Emerging Market Free Equity Index
EMBI+ J.P. Morgan Emerging Markets Bond Index
GBI J.P. Morgan Global Bond Index
MSHY Morgan Stanley High Yield Bond Index

Source: Morgan Stanley

Knowing about correlations should in theory allow for more scientific risktaking. A portfolio of non-correlated risks is likely to lose less over time than one of correlated risks. The contents of a correlated portfolio can all go bad at once, although they can also, at times, do the opposite and all make spectacular gains.

By the mid-1990s, the investment banks had persuaded the Basel regulators that they knew enough about the correlation of markets to run portfolios of assets whose exposure to market risks could be tuned to benefit from non-correlation.

There was some clever lobbying. In 1994, J.P. Morgan made many of its correlation tables available free on a website called RiskMetrics. RiskMetrics gave other banks, fund managers, corporate treasurers and even private investors a free method of assessing the likely volatility of their exposures and how much they could lose on a bad day. What better way to establish VAR as a market standard for everyone to follow?

The Basel committee at this time was discussing what capital requirements should be put on banks' exposures to market risk. The banks were lobbying hard against simple standards that would apply a charge for each risk, and would ignore the fact that some non-correlated risks offset each other. Sophisticated banks argued that the regulatory capital charge for their risk should be assessed on a portfolio basis – taking account of the observation that some risks offset others – since that was how the banks themselves assessed and managed their risk. After all, they were beginning to allocate capital internally to the risks of each business and each portfolio that they ran. To calculate that allocation of what they called "economic" rather than regulatory capital, they would use their own VAR models. Their understanding of correlations allowed them to factor correlation into their models, reducing the overall requirement for economic capital. Surely it was only fair that regulators should make regulatory capital as closely aligned as possible with the real risks in the banks' portfolio. In other words, the banks wanted their own VAR models to be used as the basis for fixing regulatory capital.

Hook, line and sinker

The regulators swallowed the bait. In April 1995 the Basel Committee put out a consultation paper for the first time suggesting that "sophisticated" banks should be allowed to set their own measure of regulatory capital for the market risk of their portfolio, based on their own VAR calculations. The paper offered two approaches: a simple "standard" approach for banks that were too small or not sophisticated enough to run their own VAR calculation; and a models-based approach for those sophisticated enough to calculate VAR. But there was a catch. The regulators were wary of the banks' tendency to be overoptimistic, even reckless, about their positions. They said they would set a VAR multiplier that would provide a cushion, raising the regulatory capital requirement well above the banks' racy VAR calculation.

To calibrate the multiplier, bank supervisors ran a simple test. They asked a number of sophisticated banks to use their VAR models to calculate the VAR of a sample portfolio of bonds, shares, swaps and derivatives. This would reveal how consistent these banks were at estimating the danger in their positions.

The results were not encouraging. There was a huge variation in VAR calculations on the same portfolio. Of course, there should be some variation. Each bank would put into its model its own assumptions about the future volatility of interest rates and exchange rates.

On the basis of this and other tests, the Basel regulators decided that a sensible multiplier would be a minimum of three times a bank's own VAR calculation.

There was an outcry. It was as if the regulators had encouraged and approved the design of a car capable of going 150 miles per hour and then put a 50mph speed limit on it. Nevertheless, the banks that led the field in risk management did not want to give up the principle of using their own models to set regulatory capital. The new market-risk regime was introduced in 1997 and was also written into a new capital adequacy directive for banks, securities houses and investment firms in the European Union.

This put an extra burden on bank supervisors. They had to have experts capable of inspecting and validating the VAR models used by the sophisticated banks. This was particularly hard for the less sophisticated supervisors.

It was around this time that Basel 1, the 1988 guidelines on regulatory capital for credit risk exposures, was beginning to look decidedly creaky. Basel 1 had served its purpose in encouraging bank regulators worldwide to care about the level of capital held by banks in relation to their risk assets. Before, Japanese and French state-owned banks, to take just two examples, had been allowed to operate with capital far below the Basel 1 standards.

Time to plug the gap

Supervisors were worried about Basel 1's loopholes, which banks were increasingly tempted to exploit, and its inconsistencies. For example, no distinction was made between credit exposure to a top-rated company, such as IBM, and the riskiest fly-by-night corporation. The temptation, therefore, was for banks to lend to riskier companies, since there was no regulatory capital saving if they lent more conservatively. Again, the poorly supervised Japanese banks were most guilty of exploiting this loophole, increasing their lending to riskier companies in pursuit of higher returns and disregarding the heightened danger of doing so.

The sophisticated banks knew that regulators wanted to introduce better defined capital charges. In the mid-1990s the culture of risk management was in full swing. Great emphasis was put on the need for an independent department within the bank with the power to monitor, assess and control what its traders and risktakers were doing. The chief risk officer would in theory have the most complete view of the risks being run by the institution. He would have the authority to order positions to be closed or hedged if he judged them too risky, or if there was too much concentration on a single type of risk.

It was a time during which the risk experts grew increasingly confident that they were getting ever closer to identifying and quantifying the whole gamut of risks run by a financial firm. After their success in persuading regulators to accept their market-risk models as a standard for setting regulatory capital, they were counting on regulators following the same route on credit risk. Many banks at the time were working on credit-risk models. The basic principle of such models was to look at a bundle of credit risks on a portfolio basis.

Traditionally, when a bank makes a loan it has decided to lend money on the basis that it will be repaid in full. But it knows that some borrowers will fail to keep up payments, or even go bust. A bank considering its portfolio of loans can make assumptions about how many of those loans will go into default and how much it may recover from the borrower. Each portfolio of loans can be assigned an expected default rate and an expected loss, given that rate of default. Simple, except companies do not default very often. It is a lot harder to develop a VaR number for credit risk than for market risk. This did not deter the banks from trying. They put a lot of pressure on regulators to allow the use of credit-risk models in impending amendments to the ageing 1988 Basel Capital Accord.

In September 1998 the Bank of England sponsored a conference on credit-risk models. The great and the good of credit-risk modelling, such as Bob Mark and Michel Crouhy of the CIBC, Tom Wilson of McKinsey (now at Mercer Oliver Wyman) and Stephen Kealhofer of KMV in California, were invited to argue the virtues of their scientific approach to credit.

Bill McDonough, chairman of the Federal Reserve Bank of New York, gave the keynote speech, looking forward to a time when regulatory capital would more accurately reflect the real risks that banks were running. He added cryptically that the financial system was living through one of its most dangerous times.

Back to the drawing board

At the Bank of England conference the credit-risk modellers themselves acknowledged the flaws in their creations. There simply were not enough data, especially outside the biggest companies in America, to estimate convincing probabilities of default, and even less the recovery rate from companies in administration or bankruptcy. The regulators who were there, especially those from Europe, certainly were not sympathetic (see Chapter 6).

A day later the significance of McDonough's remarks suddenly became clear. Long-Term Capital Management (LTCM) was on the brink of collapse, because of its huge positions in equities and government bonds. It had made two mistakes. The first was to make highly geared bets on price anomalies in the government bond markets; these went badly wrong when Russia defaulted on its domestic debt in August 1998 triggering a worldwide liquidity crisis in bonds. The second was to stray beyond its area of expertise into bets on equities and potential takeover targets. This was despite LTCM's much-touted risk-management expertise in the form of two Nobel laureates, Robert Merton and Myron Scholes. Scholes was co-inventor of the Black-Scholes option pricing model, one of the earliest and most fundamental building-blocks of derivatives risk management.

LTCM had vaunted its ability to monitor the value-at-risk of its portfolio at all times. Its collapse was therefore a deep psychological blow for VaR supporters (see Chapter 15).

Indeed, it was a classic illustration of the shortcomings of VaR. VaR only tells you your maximum loss 95 or 99 days out of 100. It does not work for extreme market conditions. LTCM's risk managers made the excuse that they were hit by a 100-year storm (a storm with a ferocity that hits maybe once every 100 years). It was a fundamental lesson in risk management which came at a time when bankers, and even their regulators, were getting too enamoured of quantitative models. It was a reminder that extreme events can knock models to pieces, and in the 1990s extreme events seemed to be hitting the financial system with increasing frequency.

The following two chapters are based on articles written by the author for *Euromoney* in 1998. Chapter 6 pinpoints an extraordinary time in the history of risk management, when the optimists (believers in the ultimate triumph of risk models) clashed with the sceptics (who believe models are ultimately flawed). Chapter 7 documents the development of the notion – thought absurd by many – that the "firm-wide" risk manager should ultimately run the firm.

6 Credit models get a thrashing

In September 1998, a few days before one of the biggest financial collapses in recent history, the near-bankruptcy of Long-Term Capital Management, more than 200 credit experts and their regulators spent two days deep underground (in The Pit cinema at London's Barbican Centre) thrashing out the virtues and vices of credit-risk modelling. At the end of this session a panel including a trio of European regulators concluded that the models were "half-baked" and could not be used to set regulatory capital.

The financial risk industry was not discouraged. The fact that there was a conference at all, organised by the Bank of England and Britain's Financial Services Authority (FSA), showed that regulators were taking the matter seriously.

An ever closer fit

The modellers' interim goal, besides the holy grail of modelling credit risk perfectly, was to persuade regulators to modify or replace the crude credit-risk ratios imposed by the 1988 Basel Accord on capital adequacy. The accord demands an across-the-board capital/risk assets ratio of 8%, which is acknowledged to have forced most banks to stock up on capital – good. But the risk weightings are absurd for today's conditions; for example, they are five times more favourable to an OECD bank, however poorly rated, than to a non-bank company, even if it is AAA rated – bad. Regulators acknowledged that this needed to be fixed, but they were not convinced that credit-risk models were the way to go.

The modellers wanted regulators to apply the principle – which they had already accepted in 1997 in the case of market risk – that banks' internal risk models should be used to help determine a level of regulatory capital for credit risk. This would allow banks to benefit from the portfolio effect of diversified credit risk, which the models were designed to identify, and to reduce their regulatory capital accordingly. It would also better identify concentrations of risk, and in some areas indicate that an increase in regulatory capital might be required, the modellers hastened to point out. So the aim was not less prudence, but a closer fit between what banks calculate they need as economic capital and the capital requirement set by regulators.

But there was heavy scepticism among the European regulators, who form a majority on the Basel Committee on Banking Supervision. A unanimous vote is needed to change the Basel capital accords, although ironically they carry no statutory weight; they are merely recommendations for minimum standards which bank supervisors around the world can accept, or reject, or strengthen. The British authorities, for example, have more stringent standards. "No bank in Britain has its regulatory capital set at 8%, it's always more," said Oliver Page, in charge of complex group supervision at the FSA. To confuse matters, EU banks must comply with the EU capital adequacy directive (CAD), which partly conflicts with the Basel capital standards.

Convincing the regulators

The modellers knew that they would have a battle to persuade the regulators of their case. Continental European regulators were particularly sceptical. British and American regulators were regarded as more friendly and the US Federal Reserve Board and the Bank of England had done extensive comparative studies of the better-known credit-risk models.

The Barbican conference mostly examined the robustness of credit-risk models and whether they could be used, beyond risk management, to set regulatory capital.

The four best-known models on offer were (and still are) CreditMetrics (developed by J.P. Morgan), CreditRisk+ (Credit Suisse, an investment banking firm), KMV (KMV Corporation, a developer of credit-risk measurement software) and CreditPortfolioView (McKinsey & Co, a consulting firm). Each had its strengths and weaknesses, if not downright flaws, as several speakers pointed out.

A credit-risk model is designed to calculate the probability of default or a rating downgrade, or both, and the likely recovery of assets after a default or bankruptcy. The model does this either for portfolios of credits averaged according to rating bands or by individual obligor based on its asset value and price volatility.

CreditMetrics

The earliest popular model, CreditMetrics is based on historical analysis of transitions from one credit rating to another (including the transition to default). It makes several assumptions:

- that credits within the same rating band have the same risk, although it can vary by business sector;

- that interest-rate changes have no impact on credit risk;
- that equity price is a good proxy for asset value;
- that macroeconomic factors such as unemployment and GDP growth have no impact on credit risk.

This means that CreditMetrics can "allow one to identify trading opportunities in the loan/bond portfolio, where concentration and overall risk can be reduced without affecting expected profits", said Robert Mark, executive vice-president for treasury and risk management at the CIBC in Toronto. It cannot handle the credit risk of collateralised loan or mortgage obligations, or derivatives such as options, cross-currency swaps or other non-linear products. (The CIBC had an internal model, CreditVaR I, which was closely based on CreditMetrics and makes the same assumptions. It was refining a model CreditVaR II to handle credit derivatives.)

CreditRisk+

This model is based on actuarial calculation of expected default rates and expected losses from default. Like CreditMetrics, CreditRisk+ assumes there is no market risk, and it gives no significance to changes in credit rating. It does not deal with non-linear products such as options and cross-currency swaps. Nor does it take account of macroeconomic changes.

KMV

The KMV model is based on calculating the expected default frequency (EDF) for each company based on its current asset value and the volatility of its equity returns. Unlike the two previous models, the formulas used are not publicly available. It works best for publicly traded companies whose equity value is easily determined. According to the model, a company will default when its asset value falls below the value of its liabilities. The default tends to occur "when the asset value is somewhere between total liabilities and the value of the short-term debt", said Mark in a paper delivered at the conference. Mark complained that because some details were proprietary there was "no way to check the accuracy of the estimates". The model also assumes no impact from market risk and implies that the credit spread on a bond tends towards zero at maturity.

CreditPortfolioView

This model comes at the problem from almost the opposite direction, positing that the probability of default is a factor of macroeconomic variables, such as unemployment, the level of long- and short-term interest rates, GDP growth, government expenditure, the aggregate savings rate and exchange rates. CreditPortfolioView uses default data going back 20 years, where available, from many countries and from business sectors within each country, matching this to business cycles. The argument is that these variables affect the aggregate number of business failures. Far from ignoring market risk, CreditPortfolioView is practically driven by it. It may be more flexible than its three forerunners, but to be accurate it will need a huge amount of reliable and well-calibrated data.

Too crude, too narrow

This was the snag, as far as the regulators were concerned. Most of the models on the market extrapolate data and observations from the world's best-developed markets, predominantly the American bond and equity markets, and apply them to markets where the parameters may be completely different. For example, default rates and loss recovery from American companies, with the benefit of Chapter 11, are likely to be very different from the aggregate default and loss recovery rate in Japan, Germany or Italy. Yet these models are not sensitive to the right data, or do not have enough of it, to apply their technology in more than a handful of countries. Another potential weakness is the reliance of some models on public ratings, which generally lag behind market information.

During the conference it became clear that considerable work needed to be done on broadening and calibrating databases, and that if banks and other sources co-operated, there were many gold mines of data lying unused. Westdeutsche Landesbank (West LB) boasted a 12-year database of default and recovery rates among its large and medium-sized customers, mostly in Germany but also around the world. Using actuarial techniques and the Poisson distribution equations also used by CreditRisk+, it is able to generate probabilities that have a basis in individual companies. The Banque de France has its *centrale des risques*, a database of bank loan exposures to French borrowers, collected since 1948 with records of default; the Bundesbank has a similar *Evidenzzentrale* recording any bank loan over DM3m (€1.5m or $1.8m), but it has no records of default. A better database, say Bundesbank sources, is one that holds the records of commercial bills that German banks discount with the Bundesbank, recording the company name and credit history.

Such databases may be useful if pooled and calibrated across countries. But at the conference sceptics pointed out that in January 1999 the landscape in Europe, if not the world, would change radically with the introduction of the euro. Companies would be facing a different kind of competition and there would be a fresh set of winners and losers. This is nothing new, said Frank Lehrbass, head of credit management analytics at WestLB. "In our database companies have come and gone over the years."

Delegates at the conference challenged the regulators to help develop a global database of default and credit history. Imagine the power of a data pool fed by many banks, along the lines of the fictitious Sigma Bank's credit-risk model StreetCred40, which pooled credit data from 120 subscribing banks. Unfortunately, this excellent model was bad at predicting credit events in new industries, such as mobile phone companies (see Chapter 17).

"Work-shy" regulators

But the regulators did not appear keen to collaborate on a database, prompting a diatribe from one delegate, who refused to give his name. He accused the Basel committee of lack of leadership and a lazy policy of wait-and-see. This was too much for panellist Jochen Sanio, deputy president of the Bundesaufsichtsamt für das Kreditwesen in Berlin (later head of Germany's super financial watchdog BaFin in Bonn). A self-declared sceptic and advocate of extreme caution before accepting rocket-scientists' models, Sanio retorted:

> *You want us to develop a database, and next you'll want us to develop a model and give it to you as a gift!*

He had earlier made clear his view that "the burden of proof that credit risk modelling works rests firmly on the shoulders of the banks", and he was not swerving from that now. Katsuto Ohno, a daring risk manager at IBJ (Industrial Bank of Japan), compared Sanio to "an army general trying to regulate the air force". Ohno's IBJ colleague, Daisuke Nakazato, had earlier highlighted the culture gap by mentioning that his final capital adequacy formula for credit derivatives was difficult to display on the screen, since it was eight pages long.

But Sanio was not alone. Claes Norgren, deputy chairman of the Swedish finance inspectorate, also wondered whether these complex models were reliable for regulators and the simple rules that regulation requires. Even Page, who was known to be model-friendly, drew gasps from delegates when he declared: "Some of the issues raised by credit-risk models just may not be soluble for regulatory capital purposes." Models may be good for credit-risk management but, he warned, "we [the regulators] focus very much on the tails of distribution, you [the banks] focus on the centre of the distribution".

A member of the same panel, Joe Rickenbacher of UBS, also pronounced himself a sceptic and called for more liquidity (of credit instruments) as a means of risk reduction, and "first and foremost, data collection, and calibration of credit ratings around the world".

In for the long haul

This practical talk may have upset those modellers in search of the holy grail. But one delegate reminded everyone that the near-term goal was "not competing with some Platonic ideal: we're competing with the 1988 Basel Accord". Even regulators agreed that this was not much of a contest. Bill McDonough, chairman of the New York Federal Reserve, had predicted earlier that a change to the accord was likely to come "in the next one to two years". He also admitted:

> *Whatever we choose as a direction for future capital requirements is likely to be imperfect and will eventually need to be replaced, no doubt sooner than we would like.*

(A compromise seemed to be developing a few years later during negotiations for a new Basel accord: Basel 2. Sophisticated banks were being allowed to use their own internal credit ratings to assess the riskiness of companies. This would also include their ratings for bundles of credit risks that were repackaged as securities, so-called collateralised debt obligations. So within five years the banks were moving towards their own desired solution.)

However, complex global banks were kidding themselves if they thought their endeavours would allow them to carry less regulatory capital overall. Daniel Zuberbühler, regulator of "systemic" giants Credit Suisse and UBS, was not prepared to compromise. "Whatever these models suggest," he said, "the answer is these banks need more capital."

7 The rise of the firm-wide risk manager

Tim Shepheard-Walwyn, head of risk identification at Swiss Bank Corporation (SBC) in Basel, argued in 1998 that risk management:

- gives comfort that the bank is controlled;
- defines an operating band within which the bank is prepared to accept volatility – its risk appetite;
- helps the bank use that appetite in the shareholder's interest, improving the quality of earnings that it generates.

"It's optimisation not minimisation," he said.

This was good textbook stuff, likely if nothing else to enhance the status of risk managers within a firm. But others at the cutting edge supported his view. Andrew Cross, director of the risk management and quantitative analysis department at Credit Suisse Financial Products, part of another big Swiss bank, said:

> *We're trying to get some objectivity on the risk appetite. We're there to support business being done: risk itself is not a bad thing.*

At Bankers Trust, an American bank later taken over by Deutsche Bank, Clinton Lively, a senior managing director, agreed:

> *There's a one-to-one linkage between profit-and-loss and risk management. As you calculate the utilisation of capital [on a risk-adjusted return basis], so you move from a defensive standpoint to a strategic one.*

Does this mean that risk managers were abandoning their role, once seen as controlling the risktakers, to become the risktakers themselves? If so, who controls them? *Quis custodiet ipsos custodies?*

The principle of independence is important for risk-control functions, said Don Vangel, a partner in Ernst & Young's risk management and regulatory practice. Risk management should not have "business development responsibilities" and in most firms it did not, he believed.

What does risk management mean? To some it means risk measurement: assembling ever finer data and identifying, and if possible quantifying, classes of risk: market risk, credit risk, certain types of operational risk, and so on. To others it means risk control: the monitoring of risks run by departments and individuals in the firm and supervising the correctness of behaviour according to risk and conduct-of-business guidelines. But in its broadest sense risk management includes risk measurement, risk control and using these tools to tune the firm's risk/return ratio. Risk management can also mean fostering an entire culture so that it pervades the firm from top to bottom.

No wonder there is confusion about what risk managers do, and what their purpose is. For example, Daniel Napoli, head of market risk at Merrill Lynch, referred to the firm's salesforce as

> *... our best assets and best risk managers: they see everything, from trader behaviour to customer behaviour, and they know best at what price an asset will clear [ie, sell].*

This is true. But other firms, such as SBC and Goldman Sachs, were more interested in systematising that information flow. Merrill relied on its culture and force of character. Napoli and his ten risk managers (there had been only ten for more than a decade) roamed Merrill's global trading floors, interacting with the traders and reinforcing the culture that was born in 1987, following a severe shock to the firm when a trader built up huge losses, which he kept hidden for months, on mortgage-backed securities. Dan Tully, then president of the firm, ordained: "This must never happen again."

Extreme events are not the key

But the popular concept at the time, value-at-risk (VaR – meaning how much a company can lose on its market positions in the next few days if the markets turned against it), "doesn't pick up the losses I really worry about", said Napoli. He was more worried, rightly, about the low probability events, "such as (God forbid) a major work-stopping event in the World Financial Centre [these remarks were made several years before the attacks on the World Trade Centre in September 2001], a major credit meltdown, or a surprise litigation – the outer wings of the bell curve".

These are the extreme events that the risk measurers also worry about but have difficulty in quantifying. All risk measurers know that these 100-year events (which could happen tomorrow just as easily as in 2104) are the ones that the firm's capital must guard against. VAR numbers (market-risk losses that might occur once in 100 or so days) pale into insignificance beside such big events. "Market risk is about sixth on my scale of the overall risks," said Napoli. (Napoli himself was caught out a few months later in the Russian crisis of August 1998, when government bond markets throughout the world behaved extremely unpredictably, and lost his job.)

Extreme value theory, predicting the impact of severe events, has increasingly exercised risk managers since then. They simulate severe events either by inventing scenarios on the scale of a 1987 crash, a Gulf war or a Mexican peso crisis and estimating where that would put their market-risk portfolio, or by stress-testing the portfolio by applying a sharp rise in interest rates, perhaps coupled with a fall in equity markets and/or the dollar. According to Lively:

> *We routinely run six scenarios a week: the 1987 crash, the Gulf war, the 1990 junk bond crisis, the 1994 bond market shock, the Tequila Crisis [Mexico's financial crisis in 1995] and last October's downturn [1997]. Or our chief economist throws in future scenarios of his own: the integration of Hong Kong with China, the break-up of European monetary union, Korean unification.*

Nobody at that point was thinking of an event like September 11th 2001, although Napoli came close with his fears of disruption at the World Financial Centre, just a stone's throw from the World Trade Centre's twin towers.

Tons of capital is not enough

Stress-testing is obviously a useful exercise, but the numbers generated cannot be a source of much comfort, since they are not likely to be close to any future real event. Ethan Berman, managing director at J.P. Morgan, said:

> *Risk managers seem to think they can predict what's going to happen. But things happen because no one thinks they're going to happen.*

Holding enough capital to ride out the worst combination of past market events may not be feasible. "The 1987 stockmarket crash alone was a 25 standard deviation event," said one risk manager. Most trading books are run on the basis of three or four standard deviations, which will be breached by three or four market events a year. Regulators looking at setting sufficient capital levels are not trying to ensure that banks do not fail. As one regulator said: "10% more or less capital in a bank isn't what determines failure. It's management and culture."

But scenario analysis has increasingly become regarded as the best way to make senior managers aware of weaknesses in the firm's defences. Regulators have said they would like to see firms do more work on systemic scenarios. Christine Cumming, senior vice-president at the New York Federal Reserve, said:

> *Risk management practice has tended to concentrate on the firm level. But a lot of the problems we've had have been at the macro level – such as the US real estate crisis of the early 1990s. Despite prudence at the individual level you can get caught up in these.*

Pure market risk is low on the list of nightmare scenarios because increased computer power and increasingly sophisticated pattern analysis have allowed market risk to be quantified as never before. Since the mid-1980s financial firms have invested millions in front-office trading systems and more recently in mid- and back-office systems. Moreover, most risk managers are confident that they would lose less than value-at-risk (VAR) figures predict, simply because they believe they can recognise problems early and trade out of them. "VAR assumes everyone sits on his hands for two weeks," said Napoli.

Better to travel than to arrive

After early attention to market risk, a similar effort was made in the more quantifiable areas of credit risk, such as the risk of credit spreads widening, the probability of default by companies of a certain credit rating, and so on. Risk measurement of this type, however, "is not a goal, it's a journey", said Maarten Nederlof, then a senior vice-president at Capital Market Risk Advisors in New York. Of the attempt to quantify, said Lively:

> *85% of its value is in the discovery process. The production of the figures requires you to answer so many questions. Even if*

you don't produce the numbers you know the business so much better.

A goal of risk measurement is to reduce the number of surprises that can occur in as many areas of the business as possible. Lively said:

We have a "no surprise" mandate to act as a catalyst for discussion and make sure that no [useful] idea is unpresented.

Gathering the information into one place, as one of the most sophisticated global banks at the time (J.P. Morgan) admitted, "is not a trivial exercise". But advances in information technology have made it more feasible.

This has tempted institutions to believe they can do something else too: allocate a theoretical capital cost to different risks and business areas within the firm. In theory, if the allocation is right it means the firm's resources are put at risk in the most efficient way for the optimum quality of returns.

However, the allocation is finally a matter of judgment, not mathematics, as any attempt so far has shown. Although there are certain zealots who believe that every risk is quantifiable and can be given a capital cost, they have not presented convincing evidence of this. Mathematics has not yet successfully got its head around the capital cost of legal risk, settlement risk, operational risk, fraud, walkout of personnel, or any string of low probability events, such as war, earthquake, a systemic financial shock or a body blow to a firm's reputation.

Despite this limitation, leading financial firms always maintain that they are getting closer to defining what is the right allocation of economic capital to different businesses. Some operational risks, such as errors and failed trades, do have a data history to work from. Since 1998 co-ordinated efforts have been made to gather more such information and share it. The dilemma, however, is that the more this information is shared, the less of a competitive advantage there is in collecting your own data.

Internal market

A firm must develop a "shadow risk-pricing mechanism" to calculate the risk/return on its various businesses. This is what Shepheard-Walwyn and Robert Litterman, risk managers at SBC and Goldman Sachs respectively, argued in a joint paper in 1998.[4] The capital which management then selects should, the paper says, "be greater than the capital which the regulators require, which in turn must be greater than the minimum capital which is produced by the risk modelling process". The authors devise an equation based on the standard Sharpe (risk/return) ratio for investment portfolios. Extrapolating from the aggregate risks run by the firm, they show that a Sharpe ratio for the entire risk of the firm can be arrived at and that appropriate risk charges to the business areas can be made. The Sharpe ratios for the different businesses and the shadow risk prices can be used to determine which businesses are producing the most efficient risk/return. Thus risk pricing can assist decisions on how much to invest in which businesses. Risk management becomes a business driver.

The authors admit that "much more work remains to be done on risk measurement" before firms can factor in operational risks "which impact the firm's volatility of earnings ... and where measurement techniques are relatively underdeveloped at present". But risk pricing is better than capital allocation, they conclude, because it recognises correlation between the different risks run by different business areas, and because it does not demand precise measurement of all risk factors. New factors can be added as they become better quantified.

For Bob Gumerlock, a former risk controller at SBC, this is what a firm's chief financial officer "always wanted to do, but he never had the tools".

Risk-adjusted pay packets

Setting a risk/return on businesses is important for another reason: rewarding the risktakers (traders) on the basis not just of their earnings, but also on returns adjusted by the losses the entire firm might incur and by other business considerations. "If compensation is based [just] on trading revenues," said Napoli, "I guarantee bad behaviour." He explained that Merrill Lynch rewarded risktakers on the basis of "a partnership in business areas" and shares restricted over five years. Few but the most feudal of firms will pay a bonus related to "a direct percentage of a trader's earnings", said a managing director at a big bank. The trick is "to build incentives [for traders] to improve the quality of [the firm's] earnings", said Shepheard-Walwyn. The next trick is to ensure that whatever incentives you build are not set in stone but are constantly evolving, so that smart traders do not permanently skew their business to what can only be an imperfect model.

The wider task, outlined by the SBC/Goldman paper, is to set a firm's economic capital. This must be more than the capital-at-risk implied by the firm's various VAR models, and it must also be more than that required by the regulators. Otherwise there is a danger that regulatory capital requirements will become the criteria that determine the business.

Fixing a firm's optimum economic capital is something that has come late to the finance industry. Oil companies and other manufacturers have been calculating their earnings volatility with computer models of their (admittedly much simpler) businesses since the 1950s. Financial firms have used computers for trading and for management information systems (MIS) for 15–20 years. They are just beginning to calculate their enterprise-wide risk as other industries have done. Michael Dempster, director of the centre for financial research at the Judge Institute of Management, Cambridge University, said:

> *Banks got ahead of each other by acquiring more and more knowledge. Now the trick is what you can do with information.*

Risk managers are astonished at how important their profession has become. Lively said:

> *Something that started as an MIS experiment is now a major function. It's extraordinary. It's a new profession; nobody's done this before.*

Some regulators felt that giving risk management the status of a profession, with qualifications and a code of conduct, would be the key to raising standards among the second-tier firms. "If you break the code, you lose your status, as in the insurance industry," suggested one bank supervisor.

Flying by wire

Did this all add up to reinventing the wheel? Have the risks run by financial firms changed so much from those prevalent in the 1970s or even the 19th century? According to one risk manager:

> *One man used to be able to keep them all in his head. Now positions are so complex, no one can do that any more, not even [former world chess champion] Garry Kasparov.*

A comparison might be an early biplane, with canvas wings, which could coast to earth if it got into trouble. Now a global financial firm is more like a deliberately unstable superfighter, which will crash if the pilot dares to fly it without its onboard computer.

Goldman Sachs was apparently content to rely on its partners' risk-taking instincts until 1994, when it was caught by the American interest-rate hike. Since then, Goldman has developed what rivals acknowledge to be one of the best risk-management departments on Wall Street. Its VaR chart has generally shown profit and loss staying within a much narrower volatility band, yet the firm has been making more money than ever. "Bob Litterman has been outstanding at taking the VaR concept and getting the most out of it," said a rival.

In *The Practice of Risk Management*, published in April 1998 by *Euromoney*, SBC and Goldman Sachs (the authors) admitted to some differences in their risk-management approach, although, according to Shepheard-Walwyn, "we agree on all the important issues". SBC, a big, listed, commercial and investment bank, put more emphasis on establishing a control structure and sticking to it. Goldman Sachs, as an unlisted investment bank as it then was (it went public in 1999), had partners whose own money was on the line. Controls were more flexible and perhaps more directly attuned to the risks of making and losing money. For example, Goldman's trader limits were tighter but could be renegotiated, whereas at SBC limits, once agreed, were sacrosanct. "We can buy into the trader's arguments," said Litterman.

Super-traders or tradebusters?

The next question – whether risk management does or should take offsetting positions for the bank – is wide open. Napoli said:

> *I am allowed to take offsetting positions, but I use it rarely. I'd rather the desks do their own hedging. If a trader knows you're behind him with a hedge, it gives him only upside.*

Lively agreed:

> *By and large we don't have a central hedging function. It undermines accountability and it cuts across profit-centre responsibilities. We tend to go back to the profit centre to hedge.*

Banks that are more efficient risktakers are benefiting the economy and even performing a social good, he argued. "There's less distortion. Intermediation is much more efficient, and that has social value to the economy."

Risk managers as prime contributors to shareholder value and society at large may be a difficult concept to swallow. But it may become more credible, depending on what role these big financial institutions play in future. Will they exist mainly to cushion players in the so-called real economy from financial risk, or will their main role be to lay off such risks on investors and insurers? If it is the former, then regulators are bound to be more concerned with their long-term survival; if the latter, then the regulators might be content with big bank failures, as long as any wind-down or sell-off is done in orderly fashion. Either way, the risk manager will be an important point of contact for regulators, auditors and the chief executive – assuming, that is, that the risk manager is not the chief executive, which some observers believe is only a matter time.

8 Basel 2 is born – a new regulatory

In June 1999, the Basel Committee on Banking Supervision produced a draft paper proposing a completely new framework for setting banks' regulatory capital. There were three guiding principles:

- Banks would be able to use their own internal measures to determine their credit exposure, and this would be used to set an amount of regulatory capital to allocate as a cushion.
- A continual review by supervisors, rather than monthly or yearly reporting, would be a factor in setting the regulatory capital requirement; a good general standard of risk management would be rewarded by a lower capital charge.
- As far as possible, public disclosure of banks' risk management processes and numbers would bring in market forces as a regulatory mechanism.

The goals of the new framework were clear: to align regulatory capital more closely with what were understood to be the actual risks run by financial institutions. However, the devil was in the detail. It is all very well to let banks use their own measures of credit risk, but only if you assume that they will not twist and turn those measures to competitive advantage. To ensure a level playing field, the banks' internal measures needed to be calibrated and checked against a benchmark. That benchmark would most likely be existing credit ratings, as provided by the leading rating agencies: Standard & Poor's, Moody's and Fitch.

More demands on rating agencies

It was soon apparent that this would put enormous new pressure on the rating agencies and would give them potentially even more power. The agencies themselves did not like this because it meant they were more likely to be officially regulated. (Four of them, including most recently the Dominion Bond Rating Service, are approved by the American Securities and Exchange Commission as nationally recognised statistical rating organisations or NRSROs, but they are not under its supervision.)

So the guiding principle of the new Basel framework (dubbed Basel 2), more accurate credit analysis, looked as though it could be self-defeating. The circular argument went as follows: the best measures of credit risk are the banks' own internal measures; but they can hardly be trusted not to monkey with these internal measures, unless they are benchmarked. So regulators have to specify what is the benchmark.

In the years between 1998 and 2003 the draft Basel framework lurched through several incarnations. There was also a succession of "quantitative impact studies", which attempted to measure whether the new framework would charge banks more, or less, regulatory capital than the 1988 Basel accord (Basel 1). The aim was to keep the overall capital charge about the same, but also to give banks an incentive to develop better – and better disclosed – risk management. Besides the mainstream fuss about internal credit ratings, there were other arguments between regulators and banks about the risk weighting to be given to credit derivatives and asset-backed securities.

Imperfect hedges

Regulators have always, rightly, been sceptical about the ability of complex financial instruments to offset safely an underlying risk. A bond future, for example, is not a perfect hedge for a cash bond, because the price of the future and the price of the bond can get out of line. Similarly, a credit derivative, such as a credit-default swap, may not provide perfect protection against the default of a corporate name. There could be a flaw in the documentation, or a mismatch in the maturity of the derivative and the underlying asset. (A credit-default swap is a form of credit insurance on a specified credit risk. In the case of a credit event, such as a default, the default protection seller should pay the buyer of protection 100% and then attempt to recover value from the defaulting company.)

In the case of the collapse of Enron, an American energy-trading giant, in late 2001, most of the credit-default swaps written on Enron's name worked, and the buyers of protection were paid in full. However, J.P. Morgan bought around $1 billion worth of protection on Enron's name from 11 insurance companies in the form of a surety bond. When Enron went bust the insurers refused to pay up on the surety bond, claiming that Enron and J.P. Morgan had colluded to disguise a loan as a commodity contract. In the end, after a couple of weeks in court in early 2003, the insurers agreed to pay J.P. Morgan 60% of the claim. This is a good illustration of why regulators, and banks themselves, would be foolish to assume that a risk position and an offsetting hedge are totally risk-free. Time and again they prove not to be.

In the case of Basel 2, the regulators began by demanding an add-on

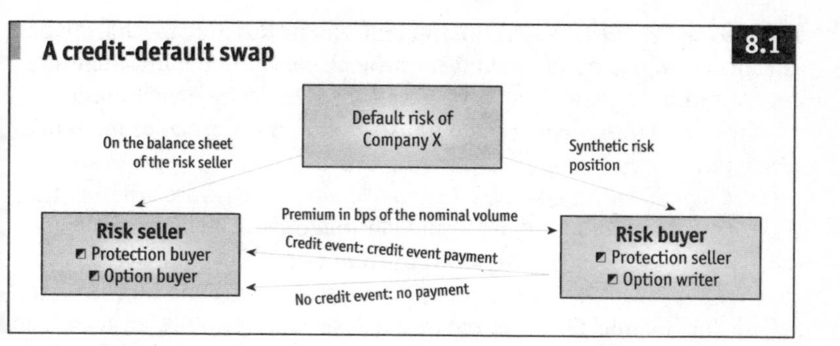

factor, called w, for any position that involved a securitisation or a complex derivative. After three years of wrangling, however, the regulators agreed that the w factor would not be a simple multiple or add-on, but it would be dealt with according to the second principle, continual supervision. The risk weighting would depend on the supervisor's view of the bank's ability to manage the risk.

Stirring in operational risk

A further important innovation in the Basel 2 framework was the attempt to factor in so-called "operational risk". Operational risk means anything from small incidents, such as failed trades, loss of documents, power cuts and strikes, to traumatic events, such as bomb attacks, fires, fraud and rogue trading. All of these incur losses with varying frequency and severity. Logically, a bank should hold capital to cushion the effect of such events. But the question is how much: how should the probability of loss and the cost of capital be quantified? Basel 2 wanted to add a capital charge for operational risk, to be based on a consensus of calculations done by the banks themselves.

Work had already been done on calculating operational risk. Some of the quantification – of low-cost, high-frequency events, such as failed trades – is quite straightforward. Most banks and most markets suffer a level of failed trades and other minor operational failures. Bankers Trust had pioneered such calculations in the early 1990s, building up a database of operational losses. Some Bankers Trust alumni later formed MORE, building on the old Bankers Trust database, which is now used by an operational risk software resource called OpVAR, a subsidiary of Fitch.

Inspired by such endeavours, the Basel committee boldly wrote operational risk into Basel 2. But in early conversations with banks it soon became clear that before anything else the parameters of operational risk had to be defined. Did operational risk include business mistakes, such as setting up a branch in the wrong place, and did it include loss of reputation, surely the most expensive failure of all?

The Basel committee and the banks took 18 months to come up with a definition:

> *The risk of loss resulting from inadequate or failed internal processes, people and systems or from external events.*

It did not include business risk, since this was regarded as a natural exposure if a financial institution is in business at all. Nor did it include reputation risk, since, they argued, safeguarding reputation is implicit in all attempts to manage operational and other risks.

Defining operational risk did not bring banks much closer to quantifying it, especially the high-cost, low-frequency events such as fraud, bomb attacks and rogue trading. In the end the Basel committee took the easier option, as it did with securitisation, of making the capital charge for operational risk a subjective one, dependent on continual review by supervisors.

A useful exercise

The Basel 2 process certainly encouraged the regulators and the banks to go through many useful exercises in identifying and quantifying risk. It is unlikely that they got much nearer to making the financial system overall a safer place, however. There is little evidence that addressing risk in one part of the financial system does much more than push the risk into another part. Since the world financial system is all part of the same supertanker, the integrity of some or most of its hull, and a separation into compartments, does not mean it will not be holed below the waterline somewhere else.

For example, take the insurance industry. In 2002 and early 2003, the investment portfolios of many insurance companies were hit by falls in the equity markets and by an increase in corporate defaults. They were hit by corporate defaults, particularly in America, because they had for the past five or six years been increasing their exposure to corporate credit risk. The banks, since around 1996, had developed techniques, mainly credit-default swaps and asset-backed securities, which transferred the credit risk out of their loan books and bond portfolios to other investors. This was good for the banking system, it transpired, but not so good for insurance companies, pension funds and mutual funds, which

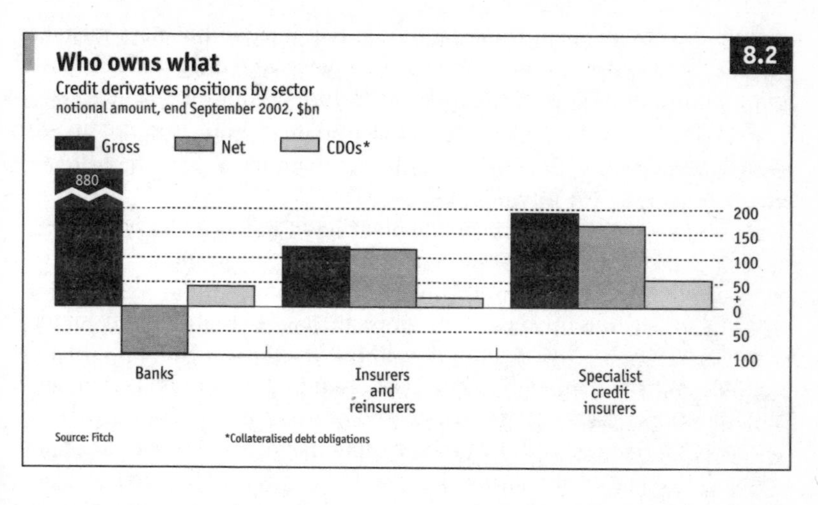

sought above-average returns by investing in these new credit-sensitive structures.

The transfer of credit risk from banks to insurers and other investors raises a fundamental question about the nature and function of a national or international banking system. Usually, bank deposits are insured. There is also an actual or implicit lender of last resort, in the form of a central bank or national treasury. Historically, banks have been a first line of defence against financial crisis, cushioning the rest of the economy from severe economic shocks. Certainly the Japanese banks, and to some extent the German banks, have even recently performed this function. But the modern, possibly Anglo-Saxon, approach to the risk management of banks does not take into account such a social function, or the ghostly presence of a lender of last resort. According to the principle of Basel 2, banks must stand on their own merits or die.

This may be a good principle, but it is gradually changing the nature of the world financial system. The concern of financial regulators is becoming much more the health of the financial system as a whole rather than that of individual regulated banks. Ultimately, it implies that the failure of a bank, an insurance company or an investment fund should not be prevented if that institution has been mismanaged. The financial system is being redesigned so that it can tolerate the failure of even its biggest bank. This is the landscape that financial regulators are groping towards. The process has huge implications for the future risk management of banks, securities firms, exchanges, investment vehicles and all other financial institutions. There should in future be much more awareness of counterparty risk, and even of the relationship between a counterparty and other counterparties. The guiding principle for doing business with anyone, from the biggest financial conglomerate to the insurance salesman, will be, as perhaps it should always have been, *caveat emptor*: let the buyer beware.

However, because of the special position of banks as takers of retail deposits and as an integral part of the payment system, and because some of the biggest also handle huge volumes of securities trades, there will always be some concern about the effect of bank failure on the system as a whole. Gridlock in the financial system is the nightmare that has haunted regulators since July 1974, when Bankhaus Herstatt was shut down in Germany. Incomplete foreign-exchange deals led to a panic in the international markets which took days to sort out. That kind of panic has been avoided since, even in the aftermath of the terrorist attacks in New York on September 11th 2001. Although a major New York clearing bank, Bank of New York, was unable to settle securities trades for several days afterwards, the system survived and a liquidity crunch was avoided.

The Basel 2 framework aims to encourage banks to identify and address the threats to their own survival. It is trying to create a mechanism as close to market realities as possible. But it falls short of leaving banks entirely to the mercy of market forces. Its attempt to harness market forces is limited to requiring more disclosure by banks.

Some pundits would have liked to see Basel 2 go the whole hog with a framework that lets banks live or die by market forces alone. There were two main sets of proposals to this end: one involved so-called pre-commitment, the other the use of banks' subordinated debt.

Pre-commitment

Pre-commitment was first suggested in 1997 by Paul Kupiec and James O'Brien,[5] researchers at the US Federal Reserve Board. Since banks are getting so good at identifying their risks, they argued, they should be able to predict their likely future losses. So why not let them put their money where their mouth is? The bank stipulates its maximum likely loss for the year from credit defaults, market risks and other factors, and sets its own regulatory capital cushion to exceed that figure. If its losses stay within the predicted range, this raises its credibility with the market and with supervisors, and it may continue to set its own capital cushion for the next year, and so on.

A bank whose loss exceeds its own predicted maximum is penalised by having to carry more capital. Thus banks are rewarded or punished for the accuracy of their own risk assessments.

It sounds good. For a while, American regulators and a handful of American banks were keen on the idea. But there were fears that pre-commitment could have perverse consequences. Banks might be tempted to gamble for higher stakes once they seemed likely to miss their prediction. And a bank sustaining higher losses than its prediction would be forced to improve its capital ratio at a time when it would find it hardest to raise capital. Moreover, that capital starvation could become systemic if many banks missed their predictions at the same time.

Pre-commitment lay fallow for a while, but various academics and theoreticians tried to revive variations of it. Avinash Persaud, formerly at State Street and now at GAM, a Swiss-owned investment management firm in London, proposed three complementary measures of bank capital, one of which would be the bank's own prediction of credit loss, plus a multiplier. Charles Taylor, at the Risk Management Association in Washington, proposed that regulators apply a *lamda* factor, based on the track record of a bank's own prediction of expected loss.

In each proposal the method was a drastic simplification of all the quantification required by Basel 2. However, none of the proposals quite solved the problem of perverse consequences: banks manipulating the measurements and even recklessly staking all on a thinly capitalised gamble.

Subordinated debt

Again, the theory is beguiling. In order to subject the risk management of a bank to the discipline of the market, why not choose a financial instrument that directly aligns the interests of the investor with the risk managers of the bank? Owners of the bank's shares might be such investors, but equity is not a good proxy because equity investors are prepared to take extra risk for sometimes extraordinary returns. Equity holders might be on the side of reckless gamblers of the bank's capital. What about bondholders? Their expectation of gain is limited to the interest paid on the bank's bonds, plus some capital gain if the bank's credit standing improves. But unless the bank goes bust they do not share in the day-to-day performance of the bank. Subordinated debtholders do, to a greater extent. Subordinated debt pays a higher coupon than an ordinary bond by the same issuer. The higher coupon rewards the holder for the higher risk. Subordinated debtholders are lower down the pecking order in a bankruptcy, and a bank can even pass on coupon payments in a bad year. So subordinated debtholders should in theory be closely monitoring the bank's risktaking. The secondary market price of the subordinated debt should reflect daily perceptions of the bank's ability to weather storms and stay profitable, and so the price of a bank's subordinated debt should in theory be a good barometer of its robustness. However, there are many reasons why subordinated debt has not become a correction mechanism for bank risk management, including the following:

- The market for bank subordinated debt is not that liquid; only a handful of big American banks have subordinated debt that is actively traded.
- The holders of the debt do not have much incentive to monitor the day-to-day risk management of an individual bank. Most institutional investors hold and manage their bond positions on a portfolio basis. If their portfolio of subordinated debt is sufficiently diversified, they will not worry too much about the niceties of one bank's risk management.
- If subordinated debt prices became leading rather than lagging indicators they would be open to manipulation. Certainly a bank whose subordinated debt price was close to an important threshold would be tempted to call its friends and ask for support, even if it was forbidden to trade the debt itself.

Argentina is the only country to have tried the mechanism. Under a World Bank programme, Argentinian banks were encouraged to issue subordinated debt, the price of which would be monitored by the central bank to help determine their level of regulatory capital. The project was a failure, not just because of Argentina's frequent financial crises. Few banks found it possible to issue bonds, so the spreads on interbank loans were used as an indicator instead. But the interbank spreads did not give enough differential information. Since the Argentinian crisis in 2001 the scheme has been unworkable.

But the quest for a workable subordinated debt solution goes on. The idea was first advanced by Charles Calomiris,[6] a professor at Columbia University Graduate School of Business. Well into 2003, a variation was still being touted by Harald Beninck, chairman of the European Shadow

Financial Regulatory Committee. It was again supported in May 2003, in a survey on global finance in *The Economist* by Clive Crook. The Basel committee, however, made an early decision not to consider using the subordinated debt idea, or any variation of it, in the Basel 2 framework.

There is another proposal to do with deposit insurance that might also serve to take the monitoring of a bank's risk management out of regulators' hands and put it into the sphere of peer pressure from other banks. Bert Ely, a Washington-based consultant, has for years argued that banks should mutually insure each other's deposits. Some banking systems do this, notably in Britain, up to a point. But the Ely approach would include more than retail deposits; it would put demands on banks to top up each other's capital in times of stress. Banks would be able to choose which other banks they were prepared to cross-guarantee, and for what level of premium. A guarantor bank would pay up out of its own funds, but only up to a bearable threshold, before calling on its own cross-guarantors. The mechanism would be policed by the banks' own Cross-Guarantee Regulation Corporation.[7]

Functional evolution

Looking to the future, the important question is what banks are becoming, and whether by transforming themselves they are leaving gaps in the financial sector that must be filled by others.

The trend in bank evolution in the first decade of this century is as follows. The big, internationally significant banks are becoming nerve centres of financial expertise and risktakers on a temporary and opportunistic basis. They are no longer a buffer against economic downturns and commercial hardship; rather, they have become part of the transmission mechanism that quickly channels changes of sentiment and fortune away from themselves and towards other risktakers. Those risktakers are pension funds, insurance companies, mutual funds and other investors, from governments to private individuals.

So banks have reduced their direct exposure to retail banking, corporate lending, payment and settlement of cash and securities, and other forms of repetitive or long-term risk. They have increased or retained their involvement in giving financial advice and fee-based corporate finance (capital markets origination, mergers and acquisitions, and corporate restructuring), and in short-term risktaking such as trading of foreign exchange and interest-rate products, securities and derivatives trading and securities underwriting.

The pressures from regulators, as they developed the details of

Basel 2, have given the banks added momentum in the direction they were already taking.

Regulators have seen that large chunks of credit risk have moved out of the banking system and into other parts of the financial sector, which are in many cases not so transparent and not so well regulated. Does a robust economy want the bad risks spread over institutions that it regulates and whose health it can monitor and perhaps support in extreme situations? Or is it better served if these risks are held by entities whose health or sickness has less immediate effect on the efficient working of the financial sector: payments, clearing and settlement, interbank lending and general liquidity? Time – and perhaps further financial crises – will tell which is best.

9 In praise of liquidity, funding and time horizons

Water, water everywhere, and all the boards did shrink
Water, water everywhere, nor any drop to drink.

Samuel Taylor Coleridge, *The Rime of the Ancient Mariner*

The phenomenon that sank Long-Term Capital Management was a worldwide liquidity crisis. On August 17th 1998 Russia defaulted on its domestic dollar-denominated debt. The Russian rouble dived in value, the IMF refused to pump in more dollars, and many foreign investors were left with worthless exchange-rate guarantees that had been promised by now-collapsing Russian banks.

The contagion caused by this crisis was astounding. Investors left high and dry by Russia were forced to sell their holdings of other emerging-market securities to raise cash. Asian economies had already been in crisis for a year. It seemed that there was nowhere for investors to hide apart from the most liquid assets in the world, American Treasury bonds. Even within that market, only the most liquid bonds would do: the two or three bonds described as "on the run" because they are used as a benchmark for American medium-term interest rates. Trading in or out of any other Treasury bond suddenly became prohibitively expensive because of the wide dealing spread.

When the music stops

In this flight to quality, the dealing spread on almost every other asset, besides the on-the-run bonds, widened dramatically. In other words, marketmakers in these assets would not buy or sell unless they made a big enough margin to cover the risk of a price change before they could hedge themselves with an offsetting trade. In general, the wider the dealing spread the less liquid is the asset. Total illiquidity means that the spread is so wide than no one will deal.

Long-Term Capital Management (LTCM), a hedge fund based in Greenwich, Connecticut, had made huge bets on the relative price movements of many different American and European government bonds. The theoretical argument for doing this was sound. Each bond has a theoretical value based on the interest it pays, the maturity date

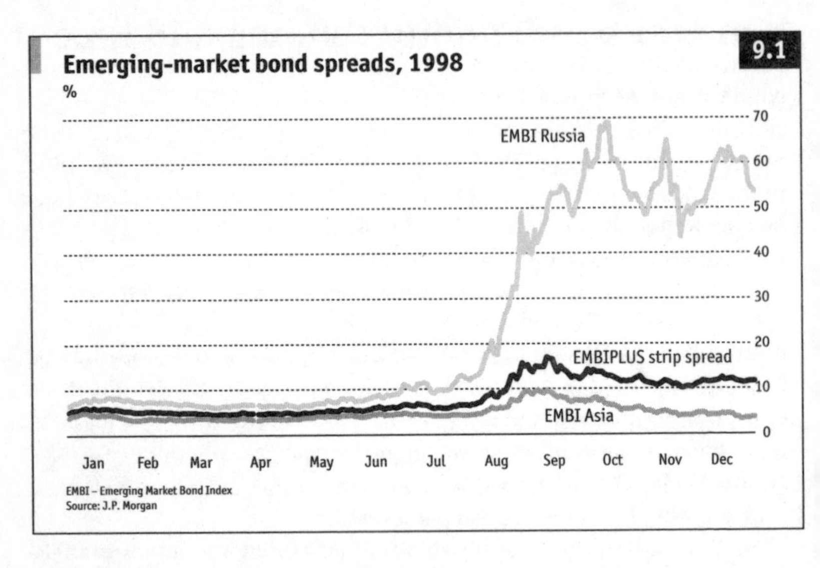

and the creditworthiness of the issuer. Each bond also has a daily market value based on supply and demand. When these two values diverge for temporary supply and demand reasons, common sense says they will converge again, sooner or later.

LTCM, along with many other spread traders, was betting on convergence between the less liquid American Treasury bonds, which had got out of line, and the benchmark yield (interest rate) at which the on-the-run bonds were trading. LTCM also had many other bets on the bonds of European governments that were about to take the giant step of European economic and monetary union (EMU) on January 1st 1999.

LTCM made assumptions that in normal markets would have been right. The European bonds would eventually converge on a single exchange rate and a more or less uniform interest rate. The out-of-line American Treasuries would sooner or later have returned to their theoretical value relative to the benchmark, even if that meant waiting until their maturity date. (LTCM made many other less rational, even desperate, bets too, as it tried to lift its performance, but these are not relevant here.)

Unfortunately for LTCM, two things happened, both of them to do with liquidity: first, there was the flight to quality by the world's investors; and second, there were suddenly much higher margin calls on LTCM's open positions. Banks which were swap counterparties to LTCM, or which had financed its securities positions, started calling for margin in the form of more collateral, to cover the eventuality that LTCM would not be able to meet all its obligations. In the over-the-counter market in which LTCM played, counterparties (those on each side of a trade) closely monitor how the positions move in or out of the money. As the positions move in one party's favour, that party becomes more exposed to credit risk: the risk that the other counterparty will not be able to honour the contract. Often the more creditworthy party asks for collateral, in the form of cash or securities, so that if the counterparty defaults it has some assets to offset against any non-payment. As LTCM's lossmaking positions increased, its counterparties asked for more collateral. This quickly ate into LTCM's cash reserves. As the cash became exhausted, it had to sell its most liquid assets to meet the collateral calls. Soon these liquid assets were used up too. LTCM had little more to offer its counterparties than its increasingly illiquid positions in securities and derivatives.

A liquidity crisis meant that LTCM had few options left; it could not raise more cash, and it could not sell its securities or derivatives positions. In the end it had to find a buyer to take over the whole portfolio.

The banks that examined LTCM's portfolio quickly saw that it had value. What LTCM lacked was enough cash to buy more time until the bond values converged, as common sense said they must. The banks that agreed to take over the portfolio (as they did on September 23rd 1998) had plenty of cash and were able to continue trading the portfolio until it came back into profit. A year later they had been repaid $1 billion, and John Meriwether, the head of LTCM (which was wound up by the bank consortium), and the other original investors cleared $300m, according to newspaper reports.

Staying afloat requires liquidity not capital

This shows how the question of continued access to liquidity can make or break a financial institution. However much capital a bank may have, its ability to fund itself is what keeps it alive. If it can no longer draw, or roll over, deposits from the market, or back up loans from other banks, it dies.

It is therefore extraordinary how much bank regulators have concentrated on bank capital as a measure of a bank's health (as discussed in Chapter 8) rather than its liquidity. Surely a bank's ability to keep funds coming in is far more important than how fat its capital base is.

An extreme example of this is the state-owned Landesbanks in Germany. In most cases, the ratio of their capital to their risk assets is well below that stipulated in the Basel capital adequacy accord. However, until July 2005 they will be able to continue to issue debt in the form of bonds that will be guaranteed by their home state until 2015. Since most German *Länder* are rated AAA or AA, the Landesbank under their guarantee enjoys the same rating, and an accordingly low cost of funds. Quite rightly, since the bank can continue to fund itself at that low rate.

However, after July 2005, the Landesbanks will no longer be able to issue debt with a state guarantee. Already that is being taken into account in the long-term risk profile of these banks. After that date, if their capital to risk assets ratio has not improved, they are likely to get a lower rating, which will result in a much higher cost of funding. If there has been little movement to repair their capital ratios by that time, their access to funds – their liquidity – could be severely impaired. Ultimately, it is not their capital ratio but their limited access to liquidity that could kill them.

Other private banks face that threat daily. Commerzbank, a private German bank, faced a liquidity crisis in late 2002 because of rumours that it was hiding big losses in credit derivatives. Soothing statements from bank supervisors and the European Central Bank were needed to restore Commerzbank's normal access to funds.

Liquidity has become more of an issue for banks as more of their assets, even their loan books, have become tradable. It means that there is more pressure from regulators and the markets to establish a market value for their assets. The world's biggest banks are closer to managing themselves like securities houses and investment banks than like simple credit institutions, which take deposits and use the proceeds to make loans.

Why not haircuts for banks?

So it makes some sense that their supervisors should view them more as the Securities and Exchange Commission (SEC) has traditionally viewed American broker/dealers, such as Morgan Stanley, Goldman Sachs and Merrill Lynch. The SEC looks chiefly at the tradable securities and derivatives positions of the broker/dealer and its ability to sell them in a crisis. The less liquid the securities and derivatives are, the bigger the "haircut" given to their liquidation value, and the more cash-funding the broker/dealer must demonstrate that it has access to.

The SEC's very different approach reflects the fact that its concern is not, like a bank supervisor's, the safety of deposits and the survival of the financial institution, or even the financial system. Its main concern is that there is enough positive value in the securities firm for an orderly wind-up of its affairs, should that become necessary.

The best recent example of an orderly wind-up was the case of Drexel Burnham Lambert, an American securities firm, which overreached itself in the high-yield or junk bond business. Drexel's flamboyant boss, junk-bond king Michael Milken, was charged with fraudulent dealing and the firm became the pariah of Wall Street. Although it had enough positive net assets to continue dealing, many counterparties refused to accept its business, and it was forced to file for bankruptcy in February 1990. Its portfolio of junk bonds, swaps and other securities was liquidated in an orderly way, with minimum panic or distressed sales. Drexel traders were in a strong negotiating position, since most of its swap counterparties were owed money and were keen to get out of credit exposure to the firm.

The danger for bank supervisors is that it is more difficult to wind up a bank in an orderly way than a securities house. A similar ostracism by the market of a deposit-taking bank would quickly lead to a run on its deposits. Once news gets out that a bank is being wound up, depositors run to withdraw their deposits, even if they are insured. (Deposit insurance usually has size and percentage limits, which mean depositors sacrifice something. Moreover, there is usually some delay before insured deposits are made good.)

The efficient frontier of disclosure

Yet since 1996 bank supervisors have found themselves in an ambivalent position. They have resisted calls to remove deposit insurance, allowing banks to continue to enjoy a privileged and protected position in the financial system. At the same time they have moved towards demanding that banks report a fair value of their risk-based assets. The first move was asking for the value-at-risk (VAR) of their trading books, under an amendment to the Basel capital accord in 1996. There was even talk, at the time, of asking them to mark to market the exposure of their loan book to interest rates. (That is, they would have to record the difference between the expected yield of each loan and the cost of funding it at the prevailing interest rate.) The pressure that has led banks to make VAR assessments has been the demand to calculate the cost of liquidating their portfolio of securities or derivatives.

The not-so-veiled threat behind Basel 2 – that the same liquidation value principle might be applied to credit risk, that is a bank's loan portfolio – has led to some soul-searching among regulators about possible perverse consequences.

Marking a bank's loan book to market may be a useful exercise to ascertain its profitability. However, communicating that mark-to-market valuation to the general public will risk an overreaction. A public valuation of a deteriorating loan book could have a dire short-term effect on a bank's ability to raise funds in the market. Conversely, a temporary dip in the value of a bank's loan book at the bottom of a business cycle might not be life-threatening for the bank provided its depositors, shareholders and other creditors are not immediately alerted and invited to panic. This is the dilemma underlying the debate over how much a bank should disclose. Obviously, bad banks, which have made loans imprudently and have little prospect of returning to profitability, should not continue to take trustful depositors' money. But a bank going through a temporary blip in the cycle that has good prospects of returning to profit should not, logically, be punished by a run on its deposits. Moreover, a bank that is punished too sharply by a mark-to-market valuation would probably have to react by calling in loans, or at least by curbing its lending capacity. This would have a knock-on effect on its borrowers that could amplify the severity of a business downturn.

Faced with this dilemma, and bearing in mind that banks occupy a special place in the economy, supervisors have tended to tread carefully before calling for the orderly wind-up of a bank. This forbearance can bring troubles of its own, however.

Whose bank is it anyway?

The case of Bank of Credit and Commerce International (BCCI), which was closed by the authorities in July 1991, shows what happens when supervisors take too long to act. BCCI's supervisors withheld vital information about their dealings with the bank, allowing it to continue to take deposits after it was technically insolvent. Wrangles over how much Bank of England supervisors knew continued for well over a decade. In January 2004 a court case began in London in which BCCI beneficiaries sued the Bank of England for wilfully destroying value in the bank. Depositors back in 1990 might have been more wary of BCCI if they had not assumed it was under a global regulatory umbrella. BCCI was registered in Luxembourg, with subsidiaries in London, the Middle East and elsewhere. The usual bargain between regulator and bank broke down because there was no lead regulator in this case.

The BCCI case raises the question: are banks special? Should depositors and other creditors take comfort from the fact that a bank is supervised, and if so, does the supervisor share responsibility if the bank fails?

American regulators learned the dangers of moral hazard the hard way in the case of the savings and loans crisis in the late 1980s. The original business of the country's roughly 3,500 savings and loan institutions, or thrifts, was to lend cheaply to homebuyers. They were supervised by their own Federal Home Loan Banks Board and insured through the Federal Savings & Loans Insurance Corporation, but the ultimate guarantor was the government. The rise in interest rates after 1979 tempted these institutions into riskier property lending and other speculation in order to maintain their margins. They could still obtain funds because lenders knew the ultimate risk was on the government. Savings and loans institutions became a hotbed of corrupt practices, and the interest due from their bad loans was often simply recapitalised. The sector blew up in 1988 and cost the government (the taxpayer) an estimated $124 billion to clean up. Several good things came out of this expensive shock. Hundreds of insolvent thrifts were liquidated. The rest were put under the Federal Deposit Insurance Corporation, and a new law, the Financial Institutions Reform, Recovery and Enforcement Act (FIRREA) of 1989, introduced the principle of prompt corrective action by supervisors on suspicion that an institution is weak or badly run. Perhaps more important, the market had woken up to the horrors that the failure of even guaranteed institutions can unleash.

The trend in banking supervision is to let disclosure, and market reaction to that disclosure, govern banks' behaviour more and more. Certainly that is one of the pillars of Basel 2, a risk-based capital framework for banks due to come into force at the end of 2006.

Capital error

But critics of the Basel 2 framework, and there are many, argue that raising or lowering the amount of regulatory capital in a bank is not the right response to calculations of its exposure to risk. When confidence in a bank is shaken and there is a run on its deposits, its capital can quickly disappear. What it needs more than capital is access to liquidity at a time of stress. Access to liquidity and excess capital do not always amount to the same thing.

Marcel Rohner and Tim Shepheard-Walwyn, former colleagues at UBS, wrote a joint paper in 2000[8] in which they argued that it was more appropriate to measure the risk assets of a bank, or any financial institution for that matter, in relation to all its liabilities, rather than just its capital. So, for example, two banks could have identical risks on the asset side – a mixture of medium-term loans, guarantees and derivatives – and completely different risks on the liability side. Bank A might fund itself almost totally with short-term interbank and customer deposits, which can be withdrawn at short notice, whereas bank B may have matched the maturity of its funding almost perfectly with its mix of assets. Which is the safer bank, regardless of how much capital they have? Obviously it is bank B.

Rohner and Shepheard-Walwyn made the point that it may be appropriate for one financial institution, such as a venture-capital firm, to risk all its capital on a few high-risk equity investments, because that is the nature of its business. Its owners are prepared to put that capital at risk over several years, without needing quick access to those funds for other purposes. Another financial institution, such as a commercial bank, as a custodian of depositors' money, must ensure that it has access to a minimum level of liquidity to meet its depositors' potential demand for instant cash. Of course no bank, except a so-called "narrow" bank, is totally immune to a run on its deposits. Deposit insurance, or the implicit or explicit presence of a lender of last resort, such as a central bank, is needed as a safety net for such times.

The strange persistence of the safety net

There has been plenty of debate about the need for a lender of last resort, or deposit insurance, because of banks' special position as part of the payment system. The Federal Reserve Bank of Chicago has run an annual conference on "Bank Structure and Competition" since the 1960s. Much of the debate has been about the role and effect of deposit insurance. Unsurprisingly, little has been resolved by the conference, and it seems the conundrum of protecting depositors and discouraging banks from being reckless is endless.

The resilience of banks, and their ability to stand economic shocks, is a public good, so the argument goes. But the very presence of a safety net for banks, whether explicit or implicit, invites banks to be more reckless than they would be otherwise – so-called moral hazard. So the deposit insurers and lenders of last resort must pretend that the safety net may not always be there: a pretence referred to as constructive ambiguity.

This seems to be, and is indeed, a fudge. It more or less works, but it is a nightmare for rulemakers and risk managers who would like to see things in black and white rather than a dirty grey.

The increased complexity of financial instruments, such as credit derivatives and the securitisation of many types of risk, means that financial regulation and risk management are trailing financial innovation as never before. But the regulators' response has been to chase after these complex financial instruments with ever more complex regulations, including a plethora of mathematical formulas and other attempts to categorise and classify the risks. This is not the answer. Nor is the process of risk rating, by rating agencies, which regulators increasingly rely on as a quasi market-driven benchmark. Simplification of financial rule-making, rather than complication, will probably be the outcome, but only after financial regulators and risk managers find that they have spent the past two decades going up a blind alley.

Dangerous non-bank financial institutions

The flashing light, which should have warned them away from this cul-de-sac years ago, is the truth that regulated financial institutions are not the only entities at the heart of the financial system. LTCM, mentioned above, was every bit as important to the financial system as a large-size bank. So are hedge funds in the way they can gang up to exaggerate financial trends and contribute to overshoots in the financial markets. Then there are the non-bank financial conglomerates, which can have sprawling positions throughout the financial markets. Enron was an outstanding example of a partially regulated entity whose demise threatened the collapse of several energy markets.

Lastly there are insurance companies, which are bank-like financial institutions with risk assets and risk liabilities. They differ from banks only in the absence of deposit insurance and the longer-term nature of their liabilities. Otherwise they deal in almost all the financial products that are offered by banks. Why should the risks they run be looked at so differently by their regulators and by their own risk managers? The rather destructive answer is that the different approaches to the regulation and risk management of banks and of insurance companies are both wrong, and both need to be rethought. Risk managers are beginning to spend time on a grand unified theory of risk management that will do as well for a bank as for a hedge fund, a non-bank financial conglomerate or an insurance company.

10 ART exhibitions

Insurance is an essential way of managing risk. To go back to basics, consider a person who is aware of a risk that he is running. For example, a farmer worries that his annual crop will fail. He insures it for a premium, either by clubbing together with other farmers who have promised to help each other out, or with an insurance company. In both cases the law of large numbers applies; the risk is spread so that it becomes more survivable. If the farmer's crop fails, the club of farmers or the insurance company pays out.

In theory every risk should be insurable, at a price. It needs only an insurance buyer to identify the risk and an insurance seller to accept it at a price the seller believes will provide enough premium to cover the risk. Calculating the risk premium depends on two things: the probability of the insured event occurring; and the amount of overall premium taken in relation to all the risks the insurer is covering.

For centuries insurance companies have applied actuarial science to calculate premiums. Actuarial science is an analysis of the probability of an event occurring based on the distribution of similar past events. So, for example, a life insurance company will calculate the premium to insure the life of a 44-year-old coalminer in Durham based on the record of life expectancy of other coalminers in similar areas. Obviously, the more detail that can be fed into the calculation the better. Where there is a scarcity of information, actuaries have developed mathematics to fill in the gaps. Bayesian mathematics can map, for example, the probable distribution of, say, cases of tuberculosis, based on a limited sample in one geographical area.

Calculating catastrophe

The insurance industry used Bayesian inference and other techniques to calculate probabilities where little information was available. How many earthquakes are there a year in the world? How many historically have there been in California? In the absence of convincing geological methods to predict earthquakes, statistics have to do instead. On the basis of a handful of data points, insurance companies write insurance cover for extreme events such as earthquakes, hurricanes, shipwrecks and plane crashes.

Mostly, they rely on the observation that these extreme events do not happen often. If they spread their insurance cover over enough rare but high-loss events and take a hefty premium for each eventuality, in theory they should have taken enough premium to cover those that do occur. This is known as diversification. Insurance companies can protect themselves further by delaying the payout after an extreme event. They may be able to spread payments into the future or play for time by contesting the claims. If more extreme events than they anticipated occur, they can adjust for the future by putting up their premiums. After the terrorist attacks of September 11th 2001, the insurance industry was faced with heavy payouts for the victims and the material damage. But the premiums that insurance companies could now charge for aircraft insurance and catastrophe insurance generally rose steeply. In 2002 fewer than usual extreme events occurred, leaving many property and casualty insurers with a healthy surplus of premiums over payouts.

However, insurance companies have a more complex cash flow than simply trying to keep premiums ahead of payouts. They usually rely on investment income or capital growth from the premiums they have taken to add to the overall pot. In the years when equity markets boomed, they were able to subsidise their disaster payouts from their investment pool. The premiums taken did not fully cover the insurance risks, because insurance companies were keeping them low to compete for business. An insurance market in which this happens is called "soft". The market after September 11th 2001 hardened considerably, not just because of the terrorist attacks, but because the equity markets were suffering too.

Convergence on securities business

Until recently, insurance companies and banks occupied distinctly different parts of the financial landscape: insurers insured risks and banks lent money. But their activities have converged. To enhance their investment portfolios in the boom markets of the last two decades, insurance companies started underwriting and trading securities and derivatives. But not always satisfied with the modest returns offered by high-grade securities, they were attracted by the higher potential returns of securities with a greater credit risk: junk bonds and asset-backed securities. Some insurance companies, called monoline insurers, were created for the specific purpose of adding a layer of credit insurance to securitised banking products. At the same time investment banks began to develop ways of turning insurance risks into capital-market products; this is known as alternative risk transfer (ART).

Table 10.1 **CAT bond transactions, 1996–2003**

	Arranger	*Special-purpose vehicle*	*$m*	*Risk type*
1996	St Paul Re	Georgetown	69	Multi-peril
1997	USAA	Residential Re 1	477	US wind
	Swiss Re	SR Earthquake Fund	137	California earthquake
	Tokyo Marine & Fire	Parametric Re	100	Japan earthquake
1998	Centre Re	Trinity	84	US wind
	Continental Casualty	HF Re	90	US wind
	XL Capital	Mid-Ocean Re	100	Multi-peril
	Centre Re	Pacific Re	80	Japan wind
	USAA	Residential Re II	450	US wind
	F&G Re	Mosaic Re I	54	Multi-peril
	Centre Re	Trinity Re II	57	US wind
1999	F&G Re	Mosaic Re II	46	Multi-peril
	Kemper	Domestic Inc	100	Central US earthquake
	Sorema SA	Halyard Re BV	17	Multi-peril
	Oriental Land Co	Concentric	100	Japan earthquake
	USAA	Residential Re III	200	US wind
	Gerling	Juno Re	80	US wind
	Gerling	Namazu Re	100	Japan earthquake
	American Re	Gold Eagle	182	Multi-peril
2000	Lehman Re	Seismic	150	California earthquake
	SCOR	Atlas Re	200	Multi-peril
	Arrow Re/State Farm	Alpha Wind	90	US wind
	USAA	Residential Re 2000	200	US wind
	Vesta	NeHi	50	US wind
	AGF	Mediterranean Re	129	Multi-peril
	Munich Re	Prime Capital Hurricane	167	US wind
	Munich Re	Prime Calquake	137	US wind
2001	Swiss Re	Western Capital	100	California earthquake
	American Re	Gold Eagle	120	Multi-peril
	Zurich Re	Trinom	162	California earthquake
	Swiss Re	SR Wind A1	60	Europe wind
	Swiss Re	SR Wind A2	60	US wind
	USAA	Residential Re 2001	150	US wind
	SCOR	Atlas Re II	160	Multi-peril
	Lehman Re	Redwood Capital II	165	California earthquake
2002	Swiss Re	Redwood Capital II	200	California earthquake
	Syndicate 33 (Hiscox)	St Agatha Re	33	Multi-peril
	Nissay Dowa	Fujiyama	70	Japan earthquake
	USAA	Residential Re 2002	125	US wind
	Swiss Re	Pioneer 2002	389	Multi-peril
	Gulfstream	Studio Re	175	California earthquake
2003	Swiss Re	Pioneer 2003	76	Multi-peril
	USAA	Residential Re 2003	160	Multi-peril
	Zenkyoren	Phoenix Quake Wind	278	Multi-peril
	Zenkyoren	Phoenix Quake	193	Japan earthquake
	Swiss Re	Arbor I	95	Multi-peril
	Swiss Re	Arbor II	27	Multi-peril
	Swiss Re	Palm Capital	22	Atlantic hurricane
	Swiss Re	Oak Capital	24	European wind
	Swiss Re	Sequoia	23	California earthquake
	Swiss Re	Sakura	15	Japan earthquake
	Swiss Re	Formosa Re	100	Taiwan earthquake
	CSFB/Swiss Re	Golden Goal Finance	260	Football cancellation

Sources: Swiss Re; Goldman Sachs; Artemis

The aim of ART was to turn insurance risk into investible and tradable securities, so that a wide range of investors, not just insurance companies, would be added to the market. There were some notable bond issues in the late 1980s and early 1990s which indexed the principal or interest of the bonds to occurrences such as earthquakes, hurricanes and hailstorms. These so-called catastrophe (CAT) bonds paid around 4% above LIBOR, but the interest payments or the principal would be impaired or completely lost if a specified event occurred.

The bond issues were not particularly successful. One reason was that the insurance market was soft at the time. The bond issues cost a lot to arrange, and it would have been cheaper to sell the risk outright to an insurance company. In one instance, Berkshire Hathaway, an insurance company, analysed the pricing of a CAT bond involving Californian earthquake risk and stepped in to buy the entire bond issue. In other cases too, most of the bonds ended up in the investment portfolios of insurance companies, which were best placed to understand the risks. Nevertheless, one or two firms, notably Swiss Re Capital Markets, have continued to create new issues covering mainly wind- and storm-damage risk, but also catastrophe and earthquake risk (see Table 10.1).

The quest continues to transfer insurance risks to a wider market. Derivatives exchanges have created futures contracts, linked to temperatures or wind speed, which allow hedgers and speculators to trade weather risk. The Chicago Board of Trade listed a contract on property/casualty insurance in 2000 but there was no interest. The Chicago Mercantile Exchange (CME) continues to list weather contracts on temperatures at 15 American and five European cities, although they are little traded. Enron was much admired in its heyday for making markets in many risks, including weather and weather-related demand for electricity and heating oil. Since Enron disappeared, Entergy-Koch Trading, an American company, has offered over-the-counter derivatives contracts based on seasonal wind indexes at various North American and European locations. These have been aimed particularly at users or financiers of wind farms. Buyers can bet that the wind speeds will be more or less than the seasonal average.

Passing the buck

Credit risk has been the greatest point of convergence between insurance companies and banks. Banks have historically been the traditional takers of credit risk. They would take deposits from the public and make loans. These loans would sit on their balance sheets. If there

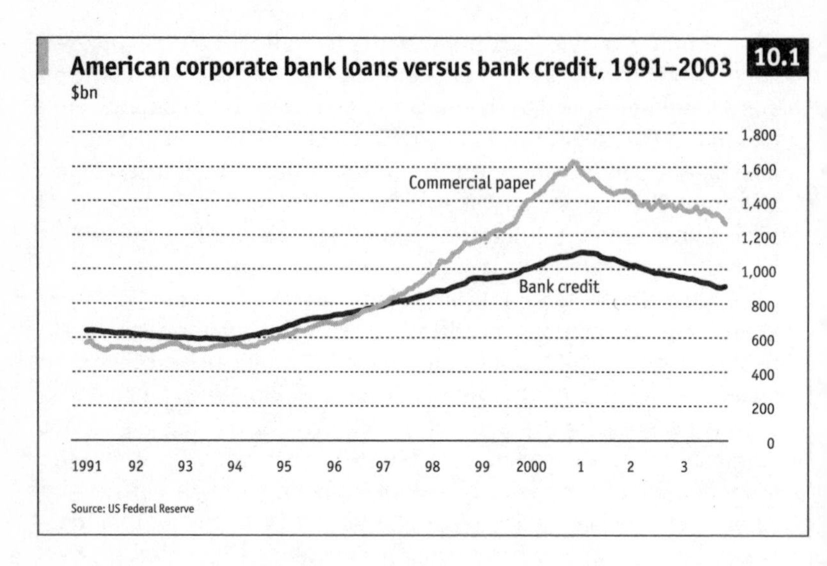

was a business downturn and borrowers had difficulty repaying, the banks were directly affected. They would either dig into their reserves and ride out the cycle, extending the maturity of loans and exercising forbearance, or get tough, call in loans and cash in collateral posted by borrowers.

During the late 1970s, however, banks became increasingly reluctant to act as financial shock absorbers during business downturns. They worked on ways of getting the loans off their balance sheet, or at least spreading the risk, just as insurance companies spread risk by laying it off with reinsurance companies. Syndicated loans – loans arranged by one bank or a small group of banks and then laid off with many more – were the rage in the early 1980s. Huge syndicated loans were arranged for big companies and for sovereign borrowers, even high-risk ones, such as Mexico, Haiti and Iraq (in 1985 and 1987 while it was still at war with Iran).

When Mexico sought to reschedule $80 billion of debt in September 1982, the banks learned that even this diversification through syndication was not enough. It did not get the credit risk out of the banking system.

The bulk ($48 billion) of Mexico's rescheduled debt – the negotiations lasted until 1990 – took the form of Brady bonds, named after Nicholas Brady, then America's treasury secretary. Bank loans were converted into two types of 30-year bonds: par bonds, which paid a low interest

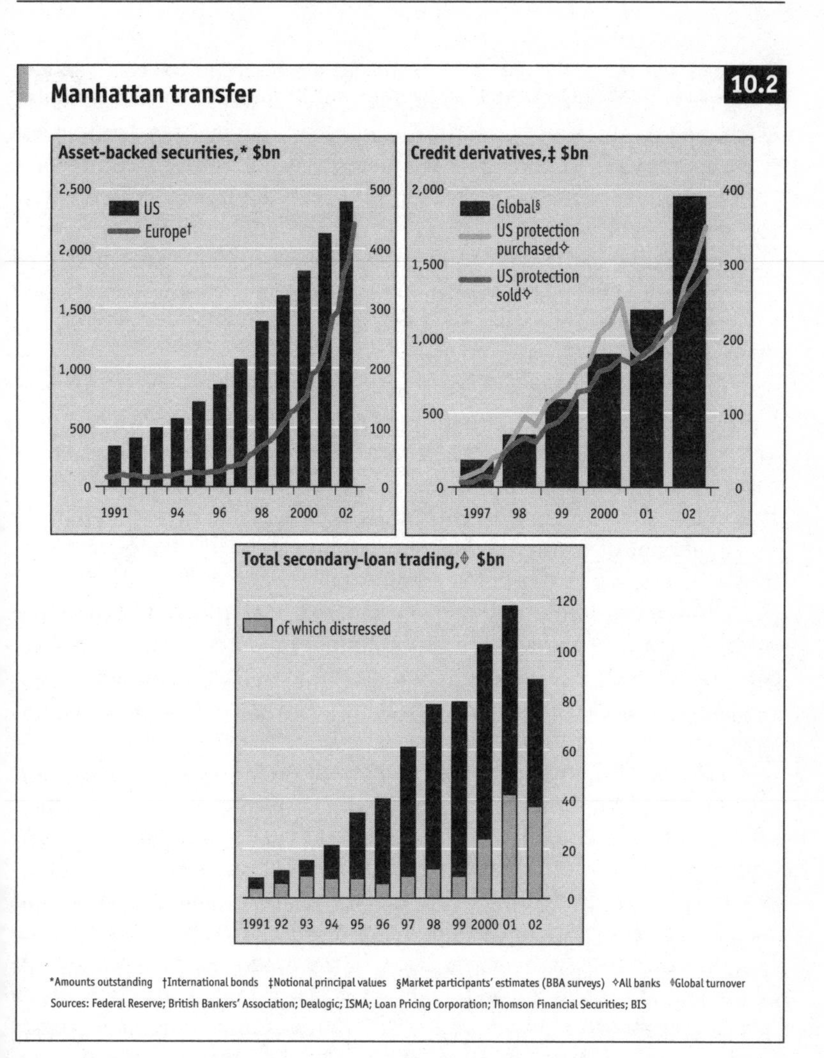

rate but eventually repaid all the initial principal; and discount bonds, which paid a market interest rate on a reduced amount of principal. To sweeten the pill, the repayment of the bonds at maturity was collateralised with 30-year American Treasury bonds. The creditor banks exchanged their bad Mexican loans for new-look Mexican bonds, which in theory could be traded in the secondary market and sold to investment institutions. Not many of these bonds were sold to non-banks, but some were. The process of disintermediating banks from their burden of credit risk had begun. In all, 13 countries were able to reschedule their debt in this way and issued a total of $190 billion of Brady bonds. Moreover, American banks in particular were lending less to companies and instead enabling them to issue short-term commercial paper, much of which was bought by non-bank investors (see Figure 10.1 on page 96).

Some banks had begun to specialise in originating loans that they then would not keep on their balance sheets. They acted as turntables of banking debt. Among the most active were Bankers Trust, Citibank and Swiss Bank Corporation.

It was a useful discipline, because it put a secondary-market price on bank loans which were normally not traded. But in some ways it was, and still is, a conjuring trick. In most accounting jurisdictions banks carry loans that are performing normally on their balance sheet at par, or 100% of their value. However, among these loans carried at par can be all manner of credits of different quality. Once the loans are traded in the secondary market, this credit quality immediately affects their price. But in most accounting regimes, banks cannot discount the value of their loans in keeping with this secondary-market price unless there is a reason, such as a missed payment or default. So banks have been tempted, for accounting reasons, to hang on to loans they have made to middling credits and to trade more actively the best credits and those that are actually impaired through default or delayed payments. The result is that banks tend not to price credit correctly.

Yet since the invention of credit derivatives in the mid-1990s, they have been forced to change their approach. The simplest type of credit derivative, a credit-default swap, is a means of exchanging credit risk without affecting any underlying loan. A seller of credit-default protection promises to pay the buyer 100% of the loan proceeds over the life of the loan if there is a credit event such as a default. If a credit-default swap is triggered, the buyer of protection has its loan or bond payments made good as if there had been no default. The seller of protection has to see what it can recover from any rescheduling or liquidation of the loan or bond.

The price of credit protection on a given name should logically move in step with the price of that borrower's loans or bonds. Although these traded markets are not so liquid, by the early 2000s this was beginning to happen.

Natural risktakers

Credit derivatives made it much easier for banks to lay off their credit risks. Where did they look first for takers? The most obvious targets as potential sellers of protection against default were the insurance companies. Insurance companies were used to pricing and taking risks; protecting credit was a new one. If they could see a way of analysing the probability, say, of how many companies out of 100 would default, they could treat exposure to 100 credits as any other part of their exposure to random events. They would hold enough capital in the form of premiums to survive the defaults and make a profit. Monoline insurance companies were already accustomed to insuring the risk of asset-backed securities linked to such things as mortgage payments and credit-card receivables. This was another flow of receivables, in this case related to the credit standing of a company or of a sovereign name.

Some indication of default probabilities is available from credit ratings. These are ratings, which usually range from AAA to D, provided by leading credit-rating agencies, such as Standard & Poor's, Moody's Investors Service and Fitch. AAA means there is a near-negligible likelihood of default; anything above BBB is reasonably safe; and a C rating means the name could default at any time. D means actual default. However, these ratings are only a general guide and are far from infallible; they are as good as the rating agency's insight into the inner workings of a company or country. Enron, for example, which cleverly concealed the size of its debt, was rated BBB by most agencies until the moment it defaulted.

As long as the insurer has a diverse enough portfolio of high-grade credits or credit derivatives, with a low statistical likelihood of default, then the law of large numbers applies, and the odd default will not sink the ship.

Shifting sands

However, credits do not always work like this, as banks have found out. Concentrations of risk appear when none appeared before. For example, a portfolio that is apparently diversified geographically could be hit if it is too heavily weighted in a single sector such as telecommunications. Conversely, a portfolio diversified by industry could turn out to suffer from geographical concentration. Recently it has seemed that whatever kind of diversity was sought, it has proved less diverse than expected. One possible reason is that investors move in herds. Today's novelty soon becomes too much of a good thing. Too many investors trying to do the same thing leads to overshooting, in credit markets just as in equity markets. The most reckless lending often coincides with the peak of a business cycle.

So insurance companies, by taking on credit risk in the form of credit derivatives or securitised loans, have to some extent become nearly as sensitive to the credit cycle as banks.

Are they better equipped than banks to ride out these credit storms? In some ways they are. Their funding is generally longer-term, in the form of premiums, which are put into an investment portfolio and perhaps not called on for two or three years until claims have to be paid. From the systemic point of view too, it could be healthier for the financial system if insurance companies, not banks, bear the brunt of a credit crisis. After all, insurance companies do not benefit from deposit insurance, and there is no implicit guarantor such as a central bank standing behind a country's insurance system. So the odd insurance company could go bust without directly threatening to dislocate the international financial system or costing the taxpayer money. The collapse of a major international bank would more directly affect the payments system, the foreign-exchange market, and the smooth functioning of international trade and capital flows, than the collapse of an insurance company.

The buck stops where?

Studies of credit-risk transfer made during the later 1990s and early 2000 showed that a considerable amount of credit risk was transferred away from banks to other risktakers, with the insurance industry taking the biggest share. There was even some self-congratulation on the part of regulators that banks appeared to be enduring the credit crunch of 2001 and 2002 without a major threat to their survival. But there was some mystery about where in the financial system the bulk of the credit losses lay buried. It was clear that many companies were failing to keep up loan payments. It was not clear that the companies' failure to perform was showing up on the balance sheets of the entities that had taken the credit risk. Many possibly did not disclose the losses because they were not required to. Banks in many countries, particularly Japan, are even discouraged from marking down the value of their loans; insurance companies in America until 2003 under FAS 133 were not obliged to give a fair value of their derivatives positions, and they have been big sellers of credit protection through credit derivatives.

With the use of securitisation too, banks and other financial institutions have been able to put off the day when bad credits must be recognised. It is done like this. The loans or bonds of, say, 100 corporate borrowers are pooled into an investment vehicle, which issues securities. The securities pay out according to the performance of the asset pool. The securities are usually layered into different levels of risk and reward, to suit various investor appetites. The lowest layer, called the equity tranche, bears the first losses if any companies fail to repay, but the rewards can be high if fewer companies fail. The next layer, called the mezzanine tranche, takes losses if all of the equity layer is used up. Only if the mezzanine tranche is exhausted too does the highest layer, the super-senior tranche of the investment vehicle, start to be affected.

If the super-senior tranche is rated AAA or AA by a rating agency, it can be viewed as a rock-solid investment by investors that put safety first, such as pension funds and mutual funds. The securitisation process has allowed such investors to buy assets backed by corporate borrowers' loans, which would individually have been judged far too risky. The pooling and layering effects protect the super-senior tranche. The securitisation process has similarly given poorly rated companies better access to credit.

Heavy reliance on ratings

In theory, this is an excellent use of diversification and the law of large numbers. In practice, it has its dangers. It may have encouraged further reckless lending to companies which would have failed more rigorous credit checks. It also places huge demands on the validity of credit ratings by the rating agencies.

All these investment vehicles, known as collateralised debt obligations (CDOs), are put together on the basis of the ratings that will be given to the super-senior and mezzanine tranches. The rating agencies' ratings are only as good as the stochastic models they use to calculate the probability that loans will default or that losses will be incurred. In practice, these models did not perform well, certainly in the early years from 1996 to 2002. In the first place, their starting point was generally the ratings of the individual credits in the pool. Then assumptions were made about the diversification of assets in the pool. Many CDOs were unexpectedly hit by the high concentration of technology and telecommunications companies, some of which failed in 2001–02.

Another factor, not taken into account at first, was the big difference that could be made by active management of the pool by an asset manager. Some CDOs allow the manager to trade out of assets that it thinks will deteriorate and to buy those it thinks will improve. In theory, such active management should enhance the performance of the pool; in practice, it has often destroyed value. As Moody's notes in a summary of what can sometimes go wrong:

> *Successful CDO collateral managers are those that typically do not deviate from their proven investment styles and strategies. Collateral managers that alter their investment philosophy to meet the unique demands of a CDO often fail. The change in philosophy is often driven by the pressure to continue to meet equity payments, to correct a violating test in a rapid manner or simply to manage a deal in a style inconsistent with the manager's proven investment philosophy. We have found that collateral managers that shift their philosophy are typically unsuccessful as they are "forced" into securities and strategies they otherwise would not consider.*
>
> *Commonly asked CDO questions: Moody's responds*, February 2001

Insurance companies are involved in the CDO market in two ways: as end investors; and as insurers of the highest super-senior tranches. In cases where these have been impaired, they have suffered losses on paper, if not actual losses.

CDOs and credit derivatives, which now total over $1 trillion in outstanding amounts, are just an example of how the traditional barriers between banking and insurance, and indeed other big investment institutions, have broken down. It is becoming more difficult to identify where the ultimate risks in the financial system lie, and where the hot spots will be in the next global financial crisis.

It may be that all this cross-sectoral activity has distributed the risk better, reducing the likelihood of a systemic crisis. Or it may be that the ultimate risk-bearers have become, more directly, pensioners and investors in insurance policies and mutual funds. This would mean the banking system is acting less as a cushion, or first line of defence against crisis, and more as a lightning-rod, which directs the thunderbolts straight into Mother Earth.

11 Sibylline books

Before September 11th 2001, most financial risk managers had a set of imaginable crises that they reckoned could hit their firm or some part of the financial sector. The list is unlikely to have included a disaster that would paralyse most of downtown Manhattan at the same time. But today's revised list probably does.

The collapse of the World Trade Centre severely disrupted the transaction-processing systems of Bank of New York, one of the world's most important processors of securities transactions. Telephone lines were down, and few financial firms had thought they would need a back-up telephone network. The New York Stock Exchange had to close for the rest of the week. New York's financial community had not realised how vulnerable it was to a new kind of concentration risk: the dislocation of many firms in the same city district. They discovered that some of them had double-booked the same emergency offices across the Hudson River in New Jersey.

A disaster like this is unlikely to repeat itself in exactly the same way. If it does, however, it is comforting to know that most leading financial institutions will be ready for such an event. A great deal of time and resources were spent during the subsequent two years on creating better business continuity systems. A report in February 2003 by the US General Accounting Office concluded that a lot had been done to ensure quicker resumption of securities trading and settlement in the event of a similar disruption. The key is the Securities and Exchange Commission's ARP (Automation Review Policy) programme, which was stepped up after 2001.

Expecting the unexpected

Unfortunately, such preparations after one particular catastrophe do not mean that leading financial firms will be able to cope with a disaster that hits them unsportingly from another angle. It is one thing to learn from history and guard against the same pattern repeating itself. It is quite another to arm yourself against the unexpected and the unthinkable.

This is where the Sibylline books come in. The Sibyls were priestesses, in Greece and later in Rome, who guarded temples, including the oracle at Delphi. King Tarquin, who ruled Rome during the sixth century BC, was visited by a Sibyl from Cumae who offered to sell him nine books containing prophecies about the future of Rome. When he refused to pay, she went off and burned three of the books then offered him the remaining six for the same price. Tarquin still was not interested, so she went off and burned three more. When she came back and offered to sell him the last three for the same price, Tarquin wondered what could be so precious. He opened one of the books and immediately saw their value. He paid good money for the last three and kept them in a vault below the temple of Jupiter. But the prophecies in the other six, whatever they were, were lost forever. Did it matter?

It is foolish to think that anyone, even a Sibyl, can predict the future. But it may be that those books contained something more valuable than straight predictions. Perhaps they offered Tarquin a way of thinking about the future, rather than the future itself. Forecasting is one thing, and tomorrow it will turn out to have been wrong. But imagining what might happen, and preparing yourself for it, is quite another. It can be very helpful to examine the probability of future outcomes.

Extrapolating from past experience is one method. It is reasonable to guess that certain events and patterns will not deviate hugely from what has gone before. But using historical knowledge has its limits: generals do not win today's battles by re-fighting those of yesteryear.

An alternative is to invent a new history: you could call it a branch of science fiction, or Sibylline prophecy. This is the application of imagination, computer power, game theory, scenario planning, stress-testing or simulation to develop parallel universes. At the very least it shows possible outcomes that historical data will not provide; at best it shows how the future might look and should make it less unexpected.

Blind man's buff

Since computers became powerful enough, it has been possible to use them to run Monte Carlo simulations. Monte Carlo, as the name suggests, uses a computer program to generate random numbers to simulate chance outcomes – as would many rolls of the dice or many spins of the roulette wheel – through a large number of iterations. If the parameters are set correctly, the distribution of outcomes will be as plausible as real-life outcomes. For example, a Monte Carlo simulation could have two random parameters, such as the interest rate and the exchange rate, and two interdependent factors, such as the level of a stockmarket index and a bond index. Running the simulation on a mixed portfolio of equities and bonds will produce a huge number of different outcomes. The pattern will show the extremes to which the portfolio might go, and the probable frequency with which it will hit those extremes.

This is all good fun. But Monte Carlo simulations are deeply rooted in the assumption that outcomes are continuous, that there will always be a market, and that there will always be a price. They do not give a foretaste of outcomes at a time of extreme market dislocation and extraordinary human behaviour.

One thing we have learned time and again in the financial markets since the mid-1970s is that volatility, disruption and correlation of one apparently independent factor with another have become more extreme over the years, making previous experience a rather bad guide to the future.

With hindsight, of course, this is logical. Communications and automation have got faster by leaps and bounds; markets have become more interconnected; and barriers to the flow of capital from one investment pool to another have been progressively lowered. At the same time the use of quantitative models for trading and risk management has become more general and more standardised. While that trend continues, the shocks and switchbacks in the world's markets have understandably become greater, more frequent and more interconnected.

Historical data and the war manuals of yesterday are not likely to help us get ahead of the trend and outsmart the future. Is there anything that will?

A healthy regard for Murphy's law is a good start. Murphy's law states boldly that anything that can go wrong will go wrong.

The first challenge is to get to grips with what can go wrong. This needs imagination, awareness of how markets and financial institutions work, and a dose of scepticism.

Laboratory bubbles

We know about the market bubbles and crashes that have happened, but this does not help us today. What might help, however, is the work of financial scientists who have created artificial market bubbles in laboratory conditions. For example, Vernon Smith, formerly at the University of Arizona and now at George Mason University, won a Nobel prize in 2002 for, among other things, "having established laboratory experiments as a tool in empirical economic analysis, especially in the study of alternative market mechanisms". Charles Plott, at the California Institute of Technology, has used students trading for real rewards to simulate the aggregation of information in financial markets and what happens when the market panics and crashes. He also extended the laboratory experiments to create web-based simulated markets enlisting participants worldwide.

Such work is a distillation of market psychology, something of endless fascination to market participants. Laboratory simulations have already helped governments design new kinds of markets, for example for the auction of radio bandwidth, electricity, telecommunications licences and airport landing slots.

In this brave new world, you can think of almost every human activity as a market in which there are buyers and sellers, and a price at which goods, services, obligations or risks are exchanged. There are benefits to be had from experimenting with artificial markets. But playing around with markets is not enough. To be useful they need to be fitted into a context.

The most obvious way to create a context is scenario planning. Get some people with relevant experience into one room, propose a hypothetical situation, such as, for example, the collapse of a large financial institution or market dislocation, even something momentous such as the collapse of European economic and monetary union (EMU), and then work through the possible outcomes. An artificial market can provide a framework of constraints within which the scenario is worked out.

Shell games

There are many examples of so-called "hypotheticals". The classic technique is to have participants and an audience in an amphitheatre or similar space, with a moderator who leads a cast of experts through a chain of events. It also makes good television. The hypothetical can be a single event, such as an accident at a nuclear power station, in which rescue services, civil defence, health authorities, the government and even the armed forces can quickly become involved. The experts work on a sequence of priorities, and the moderator may throw in new information or overrule some decisions. As with most scenario analysis of this kind, the more experienced the participants the more useful and plausible are the outcomes.

Among the pioneers in this field were Royal Dutch/Shell and the Rand Corporation, a non-profit think-tank based in California. Shell's group planning department, led by Pierre Wack, is famous for having taken Shell executives through the possibility of a sharp rise in the oil price a year or so before the 1973 oil crisis. This meant that Shell was better prepared than its rivals. Peter Schwartz, a subsequent head of Shell group planning, founded Global Business Network in 1987 with a former colleague, Jay Ogilvy, to spread the technique of scenario planning to other industries. Schwartz is still regarded as the guru of such forward planning, which involves pitching the minds of executives into a number of alternative outcomes with the use of a technique close to storytelling.

Such brainstorming is useful. Multiple possible outcomes can be explored with the round-table technique developed by Richard O'Brien, a partner at Outsights, a London-based consultancy. O'Brien takes a gathering of around 50 people and sits them in groups of seven or eight at separate tables. There is an overriding theme, such as, pre-1999, the project to establish EMU. Each table is asked to explore a different possible outcome: for example, that EMU is successfully introduced, or that it fails, or that one or more euro-zone members face an economic crisis, or there is a sudden collapse of confidence in the euro. Each table has a certain time to develop its given scenario, then it appoints a spokesperson to report the outcome to the plenary session. In this way, seven or so minds have been applied to each of seven or so different outcomes. It is a challenging mental exercise, even though there may be a temptation to go off at wild and fantastic tangents. Even these extremes can bring new perspectives to a problem and some unorthodox solutions.

12 The play's the thing

Games are usually a substitute for something more serious; for example, football has become an allegory for what used to be more violent confrontations between countries or city states. A game of chess is laid out like a battlefield. There is something compelling about such set-piece encounters. We understand that there is more at stake than the fate of a few wooden pieces on a board. In the age of the video game, the player or spectator is even closer to virtual reality.

We enjoy games. They can be useful too, since they give us a taste of real situations without the risk of physical injury or loss. Perhaps the most realistic set-piece game played socially is "Diplomacy". Players, representing countries, safeguard their own survival in the international arena, forming alliances, negotiating treaties and occasionally breaking promises and betraying their allies. Their moves are mapped on a board, but most of the action takes place off the field, preferably in the adjoining salons of a large country house.

The British armed forces play war games once a year. Two sides code-named "Red" and "Blue" slug it out in virtual warfare. For them the purpose is to test equipment, communications and soldiers without the expense and losses associated with a real war.

What about the financial sector? It has complex systems and equipment that need to be kept going under stress conditions. The personnel too must be able to perform in any market and under any kind of operational hardship. What could be better than a game to test their mettle, involving relatively little expense and little risk of loss or damage, except perhaps to personal pride?

Making a drama out of a crisis

Every so often a financial-risk manager has gone into a board meeting brandishing a book called *The Fall of Mulhouse Brand*.[9] It is the account of a management game based on a scenario devised by the author which deals with a Barings-like financial crash. Board members would sometimes get enthusiastic and order a feasibility study. Further meetings would take place, but usually in the end nothing was done. Why? It turns out that there are too many complexities and variables that have to be simplified. Moreover, although there is no risk of physical or financial damage, the risk to personal reputations is still there. It may be only a game, but if the test is good enough it is a real measure of individual and collective performance under stress. Neither bankers nor financial regulators are terribly keen to risk their reputations under artificial conditions; in their view risking them every day in the real world is quite enough.

However, individual self-preservation is not an acceptable excuse for rejecting such tests. Certainly it does not wash with the military, who need to know how their forces, individually and collectively, will perform under stress.

Mulhouse Brand was a game played in August 1997 by approximately 50 financial professionals, academics and consultants. Originally, the plot was devised because the author, who was then working for *Euromoney* magazine, wanted to write about the anatomy of a financial crash. At the time, in the absence of any live financial crashes, it seemed possible to create a virtual one. Andrew Hilton and David Lascelles at the Centre for the Study of Financial Innovation (CSFI) immediately cottoned on and organised a round table for 20 people, at which a draft scenario was torn apart and rebuilt. Over the next few months a plot was devised that it was believed was robust enough to set the preconditions for a world financial crisis. At the centre of the storm was Mulhouse Brand, a British merchant bank uncannily like the Baring Brothers of Nick Leeson fame. The extra twist was that, to bring in European actors, Mulhouse Brand had just been bought by a big German bank, and to bring in American actors, an American subsidiary of Mulhouse Brand had gambled away millions on property futures and earthquake bonds. An earthquake in California was the trigger, and within hours American banks and their regulators were at loggerheads with their European counterparts.

All the world's a stage

The game was played over an afternoon, compressing a long weekend of desperate negotiation. Each participant was assigned a role. The cast of characters included Alan Greenspan, head of the US Federal Reserve, and other leading regulators, the heads of fictitious American, British, French and German banks, and journalists to act as gadflies and gossipmongers. Each character was given a dossier of limited information, not necessarily all accurate. There were private rooms for each interest group, linked by telephone, and there were plenary rooms for press conferences and refreshments. PA Consulting Group hosted the game at its London headquarters.

Apart from a clock running four times normal speed, this was not a high-tech game. Market information was disseminated on paper press releases. Four moderators answered questions, often having to invent plausible answers on the spot, to keep the game moving forward. But most of the action flowed from decisions made by the participants themselves in the course of meetings, telephone calls and behind-the-scenes negotiations. It was a primitive, imperfect game, but it was certainly exciting and it gave players a real impression of crisis and the "fog of war", elements that are usually absent from more cold-blooded scenario planning.

An account of the game appeared in *Euromoney* (see Chapter 16) and a fuller version, *The Fall of Mulhouse Brand*, was published by the CSFI.

In July 1998 the same team, with the addition of CityForum, a conference organiser, ran another game, called *The Sigma Affair*, over a weekend. This time it was a big Dutch financial conglomerate, Sigma Corporation, threatened with collapse because of heavy exposure to the telecoms sector. In an attempt at more sophisticated technology, RiskMetrics, an affiliate of J.P. Morgan, provided a "risk room" where banks could ask for information in real time on their credit and market exposure. The Sigma game was less exciting than Mulhouse Brand but perhaps more true to life. Sigma's collapse was simply absorbed by the market. In those days, before the market downturn in 2000, banks were well capitalised and simply carved up the pieces of Sigma that they wanted. The world economy was too buoyant to be hit by the insolvency of one big conglomerate. (For a fuller account, see Chapter 17.)

Within weeks of the Sigma simulation the world was hit by a financial crisis that would have made a perfect game, if it had only been devised as such.

Stranger than fiction

In August 1998 Russia defaulted on its domestic dollar-denominated debt. This was an event so unexpected by international investors that it sent the prices of all emerging-market bonds into a downward spiral. As investors tried to raise cash to cover their positions the price of many developed-country bonds spiralled too, except for the most liquid American and European government bonds. The fall in price was illogical and would surely correct itself in due course, but in the meantime there was panic which caused further falls in bond prices. In the eye of the storm was Long-Term Capital Management (LTCM). It had been making huge bets on the relationships between bond prices, using highly sophisticated financial models. Its bets were theoretically entirely rational. But it had ignored two things: that markets can be affected by sustained panics; and that a gambler needs deep pockets to stay in the game. LTCM had huge positions in government bond futures, interest-rate swaps and stock-index futures, which by September had built up huge losses on paper.

Most of the world's top 20 banks had lent LTCM hundreds of millions of dollars to finance its positions. In recent weeks they had asked the hedge fund to increase the collateral that it deposited with them to balance the paper losses that had built up. LTCM was finding it increasingly difficult to raise the cash to do this. Eventually, one of the banks, Bear Stearns, ran out of patience and demanded $500m in cash from LTCM by the next day.

This brought the crisis to a head. At that stage, no single bank knew exactly the extent of LTCM's total market exposure. But many began to fear that it was big enough, if it was turned into real losses, to give the world financial markets a nasty shock. This was the starting point of a highly concentrated game of financial poker, which was played out over the next two weeks.

Imagine the fortress-liked Federal Reserve Bank building in Liberty Street, New York. In a large upper room two dozen or more people, representing 14 of the world's most influential banks, sit round a table. They have been summoned there by Peter Fisher, head of capital markets at the New York Fed, the senior American financial regulatory body, to find a solution to a crisis that could possibly crash the world financial system. If they co-operate, perhaps they can reduce the threat and even turn events to their advantage. If they act individually and selfishly, the system could crash and leave them all worse off.

Two financial institutions, Goldman Sachs and UBS, have been to Connecticut to look at LTCM's books. They have more information than the others. UBS is in a unique position as a shareholder in LTCM as well as a lender to it. Most of the banks have to weigh up the cost of putting more money into LTCM against cutting their losses and risking a prolonged world financial crisis.

The attitude of the Fed is clear: "You bankers created this mess by lending excessively to an unregulated financial institution. Now sort it out."

The plot thickens

Various other factors are thrown into the pot. Warren Buffett, a canny investor who once bailed out another financial firm, Salomon Brothers, is considering making an offer for LTCM. Goldman Sachs is advising him. John Meriwether, the head of LTCM, who once ran bond trading at Salomon, is no friend of Buffett. Selling out to Buffett is not an attractive proposition.

More attractive is a proposal that the banks are working on. They are discussing a safety net that would not only require Meriwether to stay and help run the show but also give him and his team a 10% share of the proceeds.

Each bank has a separate exposure to LTCM. But all the banks have a common interest in a bail-out. So do world financial regulators, especially the French when they discover that LTCM is short 30% of the volatility of the entire CAC 40 French stock index. An insolvency could severely hit French equity prices.

There is another systemic concern. LTCM is the counterparty in a huge number of interest-rate swaps. In the past it has proved possible to unwind the swap positions of a financial institution facing insolvency. It is usually done by enlisting another entity with a good credit rating to step into the shaky institution's shoes. But LTCM has no credit rating. Repricing the swaps would be a nightmare. An alternative course of action, terminating each swap, would also cause turmoil in the swap market. In the end, LTCM, though threatened with bankruptcy, is in a strong negotiating position. Like a terrorist wearing an explosive waistcoat, it can threaten: "Lay a finger on me and I'll blow us all sky high."

A people business

How does the game play out? Strong characters emerge. Fisher of the Fed and David Komansky, chairman of Merrill Lynch, emphasise the consequences of not chipping in new money. Bear Stearns, a small investment bank, which has acted as a clearing house for many of LTCM's deals, is adamant that it will not put in more.

For Meriwether and his team of financial wizards it is a humiliation. He claims that what has struck LTCM is a 100-year storm. But despite the humiliation, Meriwether is left in the game. He and his staff are kept on to help sort out LTCM's complex portfolio, since they know most about it. As an incentive they are offered a share of the final proceeds, if there are any.

The co-operation between the bankers, normally in fierce competition, shows Wall Street in a good light. These banks should never have helped LTCM to finance such big positions, but having recognised their mistake they have found a solution among themselves. Moreover, they stand a chance of making good their loss.

The Federal Reserve faced accusations in Congress that taxpayers' money was used to bail out a bunch of unregulated gamblers. But the Fed did little more than provide sandwiches and a place for the bankers to meet. It might have implied by this action that it was ready to stand behind the banks if they bailed out LTCM, but that support turned out to be unnecessary.

Things might have worked out differently. It would be interesting to replay the LTCM game to explore other possible outcomes. For instance, the banks could have let it go bust. That would trigger the termination of all its swap agreements, leaving world market prices to find their own level. Or LTCM's entire portfolio could have been assigned to Warren Buffett or a single American bank.

Big-league role-players

One challenge in arranging such games is to find people of a high enough calibre to play the important roles. Ideally, people should play roles in the game that are closest to their real-life roles. A game was played in January 2000 at the Council on Foreign Relations in New York, in which many active or former policymakers were involved in role-playing.

The game involved not just the financial sector but also trade, defence and foreign policy. The scenario was set six months ahead in July 2000. Various crises loomed around the globe. For example, Ukraine repudiated its foreign debt; Brazil's was still unpaid; there was a Turkish banking crisis, a squeeze by oil producers, mass litigation against American mutual funds with huge implications for the equity market, the default of a British insurance company and reports that Libya had a nuclear weapon. All these turned the world into a highly unstable theatre and American policymakers had to sort out the mess. When the game was conceived and played – before the September 2001 terrorist attacks in America and the Enron and subsequent banking and mutual fund scandals – the scenarios seemed a little far-fetched. They look tame now.

The financial sector has been slow to adopt role-playing techniques as a way of pitching itself forward into possible future crises, despite increasing evidence that relying purely on the use of historical data to calculate the probability of future events is not enough. This generally works only for future events that lie within the average, not at the extremes. An extreme future event cannot usefully be extrapolated from historical data. The history of financial markets is studded with events which break the pattern made by anything that has happened before.

Outside the financial sector, simulations have been used with memorable effect. A stress-test of London's emergency services, played out in the 1980s, still haunts the imagination of those who took part. The significant event was a jumbo jet crashing onto Victoria railway station. Fire services, police, traffic controllers and medical services were stretched to their limits.

A drama-documentary film shown on BBC television in May 2003 explored similar territory. Called "The day Britain stopped", it started with the familiar irritant of a rail and tube strike, which increases road traffic in and around London. Soon the M25 motorway around London is jammed. This prevents air traffic controllers from reaching Heathrow airport to relieve staff already under stress. A completely plausible error in air traffic control results in a mid-air collision near Heathrow. From small beginnings, the chain of events has ended up paralysing the country.

Reluctant regulators

In 2004 the same production team planned a similarly styled drama-documentary on a hypothetical world financial crisis. Its researchers approached financial regulators for advice on the plot. But the regulators were reluctant to be involved. They were unwilling to accept that there might be vulnerable spots in the system they regulate. In general their response to hypothetical events that might unleash financial chaos was "it couldn't happen here". Were they showing a laudable desire to maintain confidence in the financial system, or was it complacency and unwillingness to think outside the box?

Regulators are increasingly singing the virtues of stress-tests as a way of examining the extremes to which financial institutions may be exposed. But the types of tests they have in mind are usually extrapolations of historical events.

In 2001, Andrew Crockett, general manager of the Bank for International Settlements, mooted the idea of running a simulation of a financial crisis, which would involve the collapse of a large, complex financial institution. He asked Sir David Scholey, former head of S.G. Warburg, a British merchant bank, to explore possibilities. But the simulation was never done.

Nevertheless, this chapter ends with a prediction: that financial risk managers and their regulators will eventually come to support role-playing and simulation as a vital additional tool for keeping financial institutions and their supervisors up to the mark.

13 What lies ahead

The collapse of Enron in November 2001 was only one in a series of spectacular failures at the beginning of the 2000s that taught regulators, auditors, investors and others a new lesson. A carbon copy of the Enron phenomenon is not likely to happen again.

But do such events, provided they are successfully understood and dealt with, improve the resilience of the financial system and reduce the risk of further failures? Probably not. Catastrophe theory suggests that the financial system, like the ecosystem, goes through a period of stability until imbalances, inefficiencies and other pressures build up to trigger a correction, which is followed by a short, or long, period of instability and low growth.

After the Wall Street crash of 1929, a wave of reforms swept through American finance. The Glass-Steagall Act of 1933 broke up financial conglomerates, with the result that, for about the next 50 years, banks that took deposits and made loans were separated from firms that underwrote and sold securities. There were also further punitive reforms, until 1940, aimed at curbing the financial power of the once-big banks. Glass-Steagall was formally lifted in 1999. But the gloves had long been off, in terms of competition between banks, securities houses, insurance companies and fund managers, for the business in the capital markets.

Glass-Steagall revisited

In 2001, the bursting of the technology bubble and the collapse of Enron triggered a similar wave of re-regulation. As in the 1930s, it was likely to roll on for several years. Eliot Spitzer, the New York state attorney-general who from 2002 led a charge for the reform of Wall Street, was only the most visible actor in a process of change being forced on almost all aspects of finance – from auditing of corporate accounts, to investment banking and securities research, to marketmaking on and off exchanges and managing investment funds on behalf of clients. What kind of financial culture might we have when all this is done?

The standards that crept in during the 1990s condoned rapacity on behalf of bankers and their institutions and rewarded it, whereas scruples about the client's best interests were seen as squeamish and weak. Trading on the firm's own account brought the biggest rewards, whereas simply placing client orders on a best-efforts basis, without somehow taking advantage of the information, was reckoned to be "sub-optimal".

After Enron, although there were few prosecutions, there was a broad-based campaign – broader than Spitzer's – to bring financial firms and their executives to book, and to get them to disclose their inner workings, especially their pay packets. The most public example of naming and shaming was the campaign against Richard Grasso, chairman of the New York Stock Exchange (NYSE), for his extravagant payout: $140m for presiding over a marketplace of buyers and sellers for one year seemed a little gross. But the Grasso affair laid bare a deeper scandal: the excessive margins that specialist firms on the NYSE had for years been charging clients for making markets at little risk to themselves. No wonder these specialists had been so happy to contribute to Grasso's package.

Dealers in financial markets have always rewarded themselves well – after all, money is their stock-in-trade – but the culture of grabbing what you can get away with grew by leaps and bounds during the stockmarket boom years of 1986 to 2000. The more money you happened to make, the more you convinced yourself that you must be doing something right. Even those who knew that they were just plain lucky were not so ready to refuse their inflated pay cheques.

But in the post-Enron, post-bubble age of austerity, financial dealers and entire financial firms grew more circumspect about the bonuses they awarded for so-called "value creation". There was less gravy to go round; firms were cutting costs and firing people; stock options as an incentive and reward had been widely discredited. The question remained, however: was this a sea change in the ethics of financial services, or was it a temporary adjustment, until the merry-go-round started up again?

Towards greater transparency

Some changes were real enough. Accounting theoretically became more transparent under rule FAS 133, which requires American companies to report the "fair value" of derivative positions unless they are a hedge that strictly matches underlying assets. Moves towards separating the roles of chairman and chief executive, and in favour of preventing executives from being appointed non-executive directors of the same company, were well-meaning but confusing, and not necessarily desirable in every case.

There was a campaign – better late than never – that put an end to the practice of "late trading", whereby managers of quoted investment funds gave certain institutional investors the option of trading in the funds after the daily closing price had been fixed. (Giving them a risk-free profit at the expense of other investors in the fund.)

It might be overoptimistic to conclude from these examples that financial markets were becoming cleaner in the first years of the 21st century. Human nature does not appear to have changed much over two millennia. Fear and greed in Ancient Rome were much like fear and greed today, and sharp money-men diddled their counterparties out of sesterces just as they diddle them out of dollars today.

Dealing with financial risk will always have to factor human dishonesty, insider dealing and price manipulation into its calculations. The only certainty is that the goalposts move, and that new ways are then found of tipping the odds in favour of the dealer. This is part of the market noise – the roar of dealing rooms, the scream of futures pits – and the silent intensity of electronic terminals.

What does this say about financial stability? It is not clear that more "transparent" financial markets are more stable. In fact the opposite may be true. Companies, banks and insurance companies are bracing themselves for the effect on their share price of more honest reporting of their gains and losses on derivatives. Unless investors understand that this new apparent volatility of earnings is a fact of life, which had been hidden from them and smoothed over for years, the share prices of complex companies are in for a bumpy ride.

New knots of concentration

Then there is the trend towards ever more centralised stock and derivatives exchanges, and related clearing and settlement systems. It is certainly more efficient for a securities trader or investment firm that trades globally to offset all its exposures to exchange-traded products centrally. Instead of posting collateral to cover margin calls at many exchanges, how much nicer and cheaper it would be to resolve all exchange-traded positions into one net position that can be supported with much less collateral in a single place, and with much less burden on the dealer's regulatory capital. This is the trend, although prudence and fears of a cartel may mean that the consolidation halts when there are two or three giant trading, clearing and settlement hubs left, rather than one.

However, reliance on the robustness of technology, and double and triple redundancy, is increasing. CLS Bank, which concentrates all the foreign-exchange trades between major banks in the most important currencies, was set up in 2002 to reduce trillions of dollars' worth of settlement risk (the risk that one side of the foreign-exchange bargain gets paid but the other side does not). Bilateral deals between banks are matched in the CLS system and settled multilaterally at prearranged intervals during the day, meaning that only a fraction of the payments at one time can fail. This must be a positive step for financial stability. Nevertheless, the unlikely event of a failure of CLS, which is designed to be triply robust, would put the financial world into a spin in a novel and interesting way.

There are other new unknowns. What would happen if the European single currency were threatened with break-up – an event potentially so traumatic, and the notion of which is so politically incorrect, that few central bankers admit even to thinking about it? Yet the consequences of a country leaving European economic and monetary union (EMU) and unilaterally declaring that it was converting some, if not all, of its debt, and its banks' domestic assets and liabilities, into a new national currency would be a nightmare. The big winners would be the lawyers wrangling for years over who was responsible for the mess.

There are many imaginable threats to world financial stability, although the financial system has shown itself quite robust in the aftermath of severe shocks, such as the September 2001 terrorist attacks on New York and Washington. However, the more insidious, less obvious shocks are perhaps potentially more damaging. For example, take the raising of interest rates in 1994 by the US Federal Reserve, which hit medium-term bond prices unexpectedly hard and had severe effects on many balance sheets. The changes in bank behaviour forced by impending new capital requirements (Basel 2) may exaggerate the next down cycle as banks, unable to raise new equity, cut their exposures to deteriorating credits. The sheer challenge of managing some of the world's biggest financial conglomerates as they try to reconcile economies of scale with conflicts of interest and internal competition could force them to break up. Maybe the biggest time bomb of all, however, is the American debt overhang and the potential fallout if American Treasury bonds suddenly lost their status as a store of value for governments around the world, particularly in Asia.

Scepticism at every turn

Financial risk management involves bearing in mind such possibilities, from the macro to the micro. At the micro-level it involves reading signals about management and performance in individual companies that present an equity risk or credit risk. Published research by analysts, on companies or on complex financial products, may be biased or misleading. For example, a settlement between American regulators and Wall Street firms in December 2002, prescribing a Chinese wall between investment banking and research, did not cut very deep and was not followed at all in the rest of the world.

Risk management means, unfortunately, always suspecting that a financial institution or a part of it may be dealing dishonestly, or that it is being influenced by conflicts of interest, or that it may be financially unsound. Even more difficult to spot is that it may have dangerous exposures to unsound counterparties. Financial regulators or auditors rarely spot these things before the market does. In general, regulators and auditors have a not unfair reputation for running flat-footed behind the rougher justice of the marketplace. Provided there is a level of integrity at some point in the market, this is not a big problem. Where there is not, an Enron happens, or a Parmalat. (Parmalat, an Italian food company with worldwide operations, announced in November 2003 that it could not meet a $150m bond payment. The $3.9 billion that it claimed to have in a Cayman Islands bank account turned out to be a fabrication. Lawyers and accountants found that the company had a hole perhaps as big as $8 billion in its accounts, the result of years of fictitious accounting and misuse of funds by senior managers.) Smart institutions steer clear of these things to protect their balance sheets and reputation. But even some of the world's biggest and strongest institutions have not proved that smart.

Then there is Murphy's law: anything that can go wrong will go wrong, even perhaps the clearing or settlement system of one of the world's biggest exchanges.

Finally, financial risk management means a healthy distrust of experts – flat-earthers who know exactly what forces are driving the world economy, GDP figures, bond prices and world capital flows. Nothing is so certain. No rule works quite so well as the one which says that what goes up must come down.

2

RISK IN PRACTICE: REAL AND SIMULATED EXAMPLES

14 Lessons from Metallgesellschaft

The case of Metallgesellschaft contains lessons about what to avoid.

- Exposure to liquidity risk: the risk that the market will be too thin to trade large volumes.
- Over-leverage (also known as gambler's ruin): the high roller runs out of cash just when it seems that with one more throw he must win.
- Fixation with one market view, in this case that oil prices would continue to fall and that futures prices would stay low.
- Failure to control a small trading subsidiary.
- Belief in the genius of one man, particularly if he has been fired by the firm once before.
- Selling badly devised products – in this case, long-term petroleum contracts – out of line with the rest of the market and underpriced.
- Assuming that a blue-chip company is well run

In Forest Hills, a village 30 miles from Baltimore, Maryland, next to a Pizza Hut and a funeral parlour, Art Benson ran an operation employing his wife Gloria as office manager, his son Bill in sales and marketing, his daughter Susie in accounts and his brother Frank as a legal consultant. Not an unthinkable set-up in an area where staff are hard to come by.

But this was not a small family business. The Benson clan was at the centre of an oil-products marketing and risk-management operation which in autumn 1993 grew so big that it threw the entire oil derivatives market, both exchange-traded and over-the-counter products, into disarray. It also brought its German parent, 112-year-old Metallgesellschaft, to the brink of destruction.

Once bitten

Art Benson was a charming and clever salesman. He had worked for Metallgesellschaft in the 1980s, marketing oil-product contracts from makeshift offices in Forest Hills, until he was made redundant in 1988, when Metallgesellschaft tightened up its trading strategy. "It took two guys hired from British Petroleum nine months just to audit Benson's positions," recalled an oil market analyst. Rumour has it that Benson lost Metallgesellschaft a manageable $50m in that incarnation.

Benson's finest hour came in August 1990 at Louis Dreyfus Energy, where he was next employed, when he took a long position in jet fuel, which market experts were sure would get him into trouble. Benson was a believer in backwardation, said those who had studied his technique. He believed that short-term oil and fuel futures prices stayed higher than the longer-dated contracts. If you buy futures and hold them, the theory goes, they appreciate towards expiry and you are bound to make money.

In the summer of 1990, when Benson had his long position in jet-fuel futures, the market flipped and short-term prices fell. Benson watchers wanted to see him suffer. But Iraq's invasion of Kuwait on August 20th bailed him out. Spot prices soared and lifted Benson's position to a nice profit, rumoured, with poetic exaggeration, to have been $500m.

Suddenly Benson was a hero and in demand again. He got a call from his old boss, Siegfried Hodapp, president of MG Corp, Metallgesellschaft's American subsidiary. Hodapp had come into conflict with Mark Wallace, the new president of MG Refining & Marketing, a subsidiary of MG Corp, over long-term processing arrangements with a Texas refinery. Wallace did not like such a long-term commitment, but it was meat and drink to Benson. Wallace left MG Refining & Marketing and was replaced by Benson.

Hodapp and Benson presided over a daring expansion of commitments to downstream activities, agreeing to take the total output from two refineries operated by Castle Energy, in which MG Corp bought a 49% stake (later reduced to 40.1%). Hodapp became chief executive of Castle; Benson and Jo Rinaldi, head of MG Trade Finance and MG Emerging Markets, were directors. The long-term offtake agreements were signed at prices that proved very favourable to Castle; estimates by outsiders suggest they left MG Corp paying about $4 a barrel more than its competitors were paying. These commitments could have made MG Corp a net loss of around $300m a year, suggested Philip Verleger, visiting fellow at the Institute for International Economics (IIE) in Washington.

Same old tricks

Benson also returned to his backwardation game. From 1992, MG Refining & Marketing began to sell five-year and ten-year contacts to supply buyers with gasoline (petrol), heating oil, jet fuel and diesel fuel at fixed prices. Buyers also had the option to terminate the contract at a profit if the spot futures price rose above the fixed price. This was an attractive selling point, as customers could split a nice gain with MG Corp if prices went up. But it turned into a nightmare for MG Corp, since the company had to be prepared for customers to exercise the options at any time. It had given customers a buy-out option without charging them any premium for the option, or for the credit risk. MG Corp's counterparties included some that banks would not have taken.

There was a consolation prize, but only if the futures market remained in backwardation. To hedge its five- and ten-year contracts and the buy-out option, MG Corp opted to buy near-month futures and roll them into the next contract at the end of each month. With buoyant short-term prices, MG Corp stood to make a profit on the rollover. If prices sagged, it would make a loss.

Futures experts say it is possible to hedge long-term commodity contracts by rolling over shorter-term futures, but they must be spread over near and far months. This avoids the greater price uncertainty of renewing the entire hedge at a single expiry date.

Even if MG Corp had wanted to do this, it could not, because of the nature of the buy-out option. If spot prices rose dramatically, it would be faced with customers cashing in immediately. So Hodapp and Benson chose to hedge everything in the near month and roll over positions right at the expiry date, when prices were most volatile.

Verleger noted that in July 1993 the open interest in the spot (near-month) gasoline contract on the New York Mercantile Exchange (Nymex) was "three times bigger than before". In August it was more than double its level in August 1992. "The open interest is explained by the hedging of MG's fixed-price gasoline contracts," he said.

The market flips

At the end of August, with the market in backwardation, MG would theoretically have made money on the rollover: a spread of 1.23% between the September and October contracts. But in September the market went into contango (spot prices became lower than futures prices), and rollover would have cost MG Corp a theoretical negative spread of 0.39%. In October the negative spread was only 0.16%, but it widened to 1.06% in November and 1.74% in December.

By November 1993 MG Corp's aggressive marketing machine had built up long-term commitments to deliver up to 160m barrels over five years: eight times its commitment in October 1992 and more than twice its commitment back in May 1993. MG Corp's hedging position was already beyond the 24,000 contracts that a single counterparty was theoretically allowed on Nymex. The company went to the over-the-counter market to replicate the same hedges.

There are also indications that as the OPEC oil cartel meeting approached in November, MG Corp increased its bet that there would be a price rise and that the market would revert to backwardation. As it happened, the OPEC talks collapsed and so did the oil price.

A good portion of the market realised what MG Corp was doing and many dealers took offsetting positions at the monthly rollover dates. MG could not shift the volumes it needed without paying a big spread for the privilege. Cindy Ma, Benson's hedging expert, who had co-written a book on futures while at Columbia University, found practice a lot different from theory. Dealers believe that MG Corp actually drove the gasoline futures market into contango. It was a problem of liquidity as much as hedging: MG Corp's position dwarfed the market. Verleger estimates that the firm lost between $750m and $1.5 billion during the autumn as oil prices fell.

As early as summer 1993, Verleger had warned subscribers to a specialist newsletter that if they dealt with MG Corp they should have a sound letter of credit from a bank. Most dealers were aware that MG Corp was writing contracts at off-market prices and was probably incurring losses, but as one Wall Street oil-swaps trader commented:

> *There was a feeling in the market that this was the Bundesbank: the German central bank would bail out Deutsche Bank, which stood behind MG. The ultimate risk was the country.*

However good the credit, Nymex required margin in the form of cash or collateral to cover potential market losses. As the oil price fell in November, the Nymex margin requirement rose to more than MG Corp's own liquidity and more than the parent Metallgesellschaft could apparently provide without going to its bankers. Moreover, once the over-the-counter market got wind of MG's difficulties, counterparties would not roll over their contracts without collateral, preferably a letter of credit from Deutsche Bank.

Metallgesellschaft's American operation, and Metallgesellschaft itself, fell into a spiral of illiquidity.

Crisis management

On December 1st, Jürgen Dunsch, a reporter at the *Frankfurter Allgemeine Zeitung* (FAZ), wanted to check a rumour that Metallgesellschaft had liquidity problems with its oil futures trading in New York. Dunsch called Ronaldo Schmitz, chairman of Metallgesellschaft's supervisory board and a board member of Deutsche Bank.

"Have you heard these rumours?" asked Dunsch.

"I know of no such rumours," replied Schmitz and put down the phone. But to double check, Schmitz called Meinhard Forster, Metallgesellschaft's finance director, who was also responsible for the firm's American operations.

"I have no idea what this means," said Forster. He sounded surprised. Schmitz also called Heinz Schimmelbusch, chief executive of Metallgesellschaft.

"Is there something you want to tell me about New York?"

Schimmelbusch replied: "I would like to come and talk to you."

"Do you want to come at once?" asked Schmitz.

"No. It can wait until tomorrow."

"Do you need an oil expert?" Schmitz immediately thought of what had happened to Klöckner & Co, a top pedigree German company, which lost $800m in Brent crude futures in 1988. Deutsche Bank had taken over the company and brought in an oil expert to liquidate the positions. Could this be another Klöckner?

"Manager of the Year" 1991

Schimmelbusch reported to Schmitz the next day. A dynamic 45-year-old Austrian who had taken the helm at Metallgesellschaft five years before, Schimmelbusch was already under pressure from Schmitz. Things had gone downhill since *Top Business*, a German magazine, had voted him manager of the year in 1991. Depressed metal prices, a downturn in the automobile and engineering industries, and the dumping of products from central Europe and the former Soviet Union had conspired to undermine the performance of almost every part of the Metallgesellschaft empire, without the large increase in staff numbers and debt.

The poor performance had been bolstered in 1992 and 1993 by sales of real estate and equity flotations. Paper profits were created by shifting companies in and out of consolidated accounts – probably legitimate but hardly transparent accounting.

Schmitz, who joined the supervisory board in March 1992, was by training an industrialist rather than a banker; he had joined Deutsche Bank from BASF, a chemicals giant, in 1991. Although he admired Schimmelbusch for the dynamism and inspiration he had brought to Metallgesellschaft, it was clear to him in 1992, as it was to some stock analysts, that the huge group needed to cut costs and apply tighter controls.

Yet Schmitz was shocked when Schimmelbusch admitted on December 3rd that there were liquidity problems in New York:

> *My battlefield with Schimmelbusch was zinc smelters, autoparts maker Kolbenschmidt and that sort of thing. He never alerted his supervisory board that he had a problem in North America.*

Schimmelbusch remembered this differently. In an interview with the *International Herald Tribune* (IHT), he said the New York office informed him of liquidity problems on November 29th and he immediately called Schmitz.

Whichever date is correct, the supervisory board might have had a better picture if a special audit of the American activities, set in motion by Schmitz in the summer at the instigation of KPMG Treuhand, Metallgesellschaft's home auditors, had been completed. At Schmitz's prompting, Metallgesellschaft's management had asked KPMG to convert the American accounts, audited there by Arthur Andersen, to German standards. The KPMG team started in New York on October 8th, but by December 3rd had not completed the process. By some accounts, KPMG had difficulty obtaining figures.

On December 3rd, acting on information from Schimmelbusch and Forster, Deutsche Bank and Dresdner Bank agreed to put in DM1.5 billion of liquidity. The two banks, which together owned 23% of MG's shares and were its two major bankers, would take shares of two of Metallgesellschaft's most successful subsidiaries, Buderus and Dynamit Nobel, as collateral.

Liquidity crisis

When Dunsch called Schmitz later that day he was told the meeting had been "just routine". But other sources suggested otherwise. Dunsch wrote a story over the weekend, spelling out for the first time liquidity problems at Metallgesellschaft.

The FAZ article, on Monday December 6th, "created a great erosion of confidence in MG," recalled Schmitz, "and we found that erosion out of proportion to what we knew at the time." Nevertheless at least one bank, Standard Chartered, allowed MG Corp to draw down credit, as it later told a New York court.

At a press conference on December 7th, Hilmar Kopper, speaker of the managing board of Deutsche Bank, said Metallgesellschaft's difficulties were "technical liquidity problems which are not life-threatening".

But the liquidity problems were escalating by the hour. Prudent banks were cancelling their credit lines. As DM3 billion of Metallgesellschaft's outstanding commercial paper came up for renewal in mid-December, it seemed that only Deutsche Bank was prepared to refinance it. Schmitz recalled that the evidence was not strong enough for a general panic:

> *All we had looked at, at that stage, was the oil business that MG Corp had, and their clients on the supply side, and how they felt that they had, in their own words, "a perfect hedge". Now an expert would probably say that they never had a hedge at all because they were hedging different products, completely unrelated on the time axis. But Schimmelbusch and Forster really believed they had a hedge, and I think they were sincere about that.*

A fortnight later, says Schmitz, the supervisory board had a different picture. On December 12th, KPMG finally came up with a new estimate for MG Corp's losses for the year ending September 30th 1993. (Even after December 11th, Schmitz claims, Arthur Andersen recorded a provisional consolidated profit for MG Corp "by reporting unrealised – and purely paper – profits from the substantially expanded business".) KPMG produced figures that put MG Corp's losses from oil derivatives to September 30th at DM800m. How was this possible? Schmitz says:

> *It's a question of how you value put options, caps and floors. It took three independent experts a fortnight to see through the US problem and begin to gain an understanding.*

On December 17th Schimmelbusch and Forster were fired, and four other board members were replaced. Hodapp had resigned the day before. Metallgesellschaft's new chief executive was Kajo Neukirchen, a turnaround specialist.

By January 5th Neukirchen had a rescue concept to put to the 120 or so creditor banks. These included not only all but one of the major German banks, but also almost every big international banking name. Some 60% of the banking claims were foreign; Metallgesellschaft was not just a German problem.

Periodically, Neukirchen took all possible accruals up front. He put losses for the year ended September 30th 1993 at DM1.87 billion. He wanted the banks to convert DM1.3 billion of their outstanding claims into junior convertible stock, and put in new equity of DM1.4 billion and fresh credits of DM500m (a target later raised to DM700m) at a generous 1.875% over LIBOR. They had ten days to make up their minds. The alternative, Neukirchen said, was bankruptcy, which would benefit no one.

By January 22nd a deal was in place. But it was messy, and there were still some dissenters. Many banks did not like the idea that their senior claims were being changed into junior convertible stock.

In the end, Deutsche and Dresdner had to pick up far more of the junior convertible stock than they had hoped: DM206m and DM105m respectively of the target of DM667.5m. They also put in new capital disproportionate to their shareholding: DM233m and DM242m respectively towards a target of DM868m. Only the Kuwait Investment Authority put in more: DM279m.

Who knew what?

Prosecutors in Frankfurt announced in early January 1994 that they were investigating Schimmelbusch and Forster, without making formal charges, for failing to disclose heavy losses that Metallgesellschaft had incurred.

Schmitz also publicly accused Schimmelbusch of "fudging the normal reporting lines" so that the reports seen by the supervisory board did not show evidence that finance from the parent was being diverted to cover oil losses in New York. He added that Schimmelbusch, in meetings between December 3rd and 17th, "tried to incriminate Forster" for diverting funds to New York behind his back to meet the oil futures margins.

At the time Schmitz said:

> *To what extent Schimmelbusch knew the details and understood the risk potential will be found by the auditors. But the fact is, he was the architect and CEO of the New York operation. He had installed and selected the people, and he had*

> *created the conditions for them to act the way they did. From our perspective, he was the superior responsible for communicating with the supervisory board, according to the bylaws of Metallgesellschaft.*

Schmitz consoled himself with the thought that the chairman of a supervisory board relies on the basic honesty of the management:

> *The supervisory board of* MG *never had any clue that there had been – let me put it drastically – any "criminal energy" at the level of the managing board.*

"*Kriminelle Energie*" was exactly the phrase used by Wolfgang Röller, a former speaker of the managing board of Dresdner Bank and Schmitz's predecessor as head of Metallgesellschaft's supervisory board, when asked his reaction to the crisis.

Schmitz pointed out that in December 1992 Forster provided Nymex with two guarantees of unlimited amount and maturity from the parent company "which were never approved ... and not even properly recorded in Frankfurt".

Schmitz also insisted that minutes of management board meetings "had been censored in important passages so that they did not correspond to the actual course of the meeting". No mention was made of the increasing commitments of funds for futures in America, he said.

Yet is it possible for Schmitz and Röller to shrug off responsibility for the fiasco at Metallgesellschaft? The supervisory board is responsible for hiring and firing the management. If anyone on the supervisory board feels that something is wrong with the management, he can reach in, ask questions, demand reports and seek out figures.

Inflated figures

Röller presided over years during which Metallgesellschaft went from highly successful conglomerate to lossmaking leviathan. It was clear to analysts from the results for the year ended September 30th 1992 that Metallgesellschaft was pumping up its profits by adding in extraordinary gains, shifting assets on and off the balance sheet, and using many devices which, though not illegal, were designed to persuade the shareholding public that the company had had another reasonably successful year.

Since 1992, Metallgesellschaft had refused to meet the DVEA (German

Association of Financial Analysts) to determine figures for its earnings per share.

This particularly worried one analyst at Deutsche Bank Research, Peter Metzger, who apparently wrote a negative report on Metallgesellschaft in early 1993, which then mysteriously never appeared. One version of this story has a furious Schimmelbusch putting pressure on Deutsche Bank not to publish. Another version has the analyst seeking more information from Metallgesellschaft, failing to get it, and feeling unable to publish. Neither version reflects well on Metallgesellschaft or Schimmelbusch. Schmitz said he had no knowledge of the affair. Deutsche Bank Research is "completely insulated" from lending activities and "very definitely from the people who hold positions in the respective companies", said Schmitz. But he insisted it was good practice for analysts to check with a company before publishing.

Schmitz said he had judged early in 1993 that Schimmelbusch needed tighter control. "He was a trader, not an operator", was one Schmitz comment on Schimmelbusch. Yet maybe Schmitz failed to spot early enough the symptoms that this man was overstretched and that his ability was deteriorating.

Schimmelbusch had always been a volatile character. Many evenings he held court at the Isoletta, an Italian restaurant in Frankfurt's West End, hurling abuse at his colleagues and discussing company affairs in a loud voice. The more conservative members of Frankfurt's financial community did not like what they heard and saw.

But few of his critics voted with their feet when it came to lending to a company owned 60% by Deutsche, Dresdner, DaimlerBenz, Allianz and the Kuwait Investment Authority. A glance at the list of major creditors throws up only two names that clearly turned up their noses at Schimmelbusch: Credit Suisse and Bayerische Hypobank (now part of Bayerische HypoVereinsbank). The other two big Swiss banks each had exposure of well over DM100m. Hypobank's reticence was ascribed to a culture-clash between Hans-Hubert Friedl, its art-loving board member, and Schimmelbusch, his down-to-earth fellow Austrian.

The vanishing *Wunderkind*

Metallgesellschaft ran into the same downturn as other German industries, but its problems were compounded by the purchase in 1989 of two companies, Lentjes, a maker of steam generators, and Schiess, a cutting-tool manufacturer. Lentjes and Schiess were sold in the same package, and Schiess proved to be a disaster. It lost its supply network and its market as revolution swept the former Comecon bloc (countries of former communist eastern Europe). It cost DM500m and a lot of management time to get rid of the Schiess problem in 1993.

By early that year Schimmelbusch was no longer the *Wunderkind* of corporate Germany. He was fighting problems with zinc smelters, his metals trading arrangements and Schiess.

A corporate financier recalled that at Metallgesellschaft's annual general meeting that year, Schimmelbusch was "hardly able to remember the names of the companies he ran", despite the fact that he was chairman of many of them. At another shareholders' meeting at Buderus, a successful German subsidiary, Schimmelbusch arrived straight off the plane from New York: "He looked worn out; he didn't seem to know where he was."

Schmitz believed that it was in this frame of mind that Schimmelbusch looked for salvation elsewhere:

> *In hindsight, it's my impression that, trader that he was, he looked at that New York operation, which had started viable but was blown out of all proportion. He allowed that New York team, hand-picked by himself, to engage in adventurous trading. It's my impression that he lost control of himself and had to hope that with one big stroke he could mend all the fences – and in the end he produced a disaster.*

For the attentive Schimmelbusch watcher, there was a moment that should have set alarm bells ringing. At a press conference on November 21st, two days after his contract had been renewed, Schimmelbusch was asked whether there was any problem with Metallgesellschaft's oil business. His response was extraordinary: "Tell me who said that and I'll sue them: I have 17 lawyers sitting across the room."

Schmitz says he did not hear about that exchange at the time: "It would have provoked a question at least from my side."

Embarrassing footnote

Who in Frankfurt, besides Schimmelbusch and Forster, knew about the dangerous oil game that Metallgesellschaft was playing in America? Attention in Germany focused on the obvious difficulties of financing such a diversified group in depressed markets, says Schmitz.

Yet Schimmelbusch, in his IHT interview, said that as early as July he had suggested to Schmitz:

The New York-related energy trading business was too large and consumed too much cash, and ideally we should look for a partner. He [Schmitz] agreed.

To which allegation Schmitz replied:

I was not fully informed of the nature and structure of the oil futures business, and I did not discuss the New York oil operations, the strategy and liquidity issues as described by Mr Schimmelbusch.

However, it is ironic and perhaps significant that Deutsche Bank and Metallgesellschaft had agreed in February 1993 to market jointly in Europe the very oil risk management product that was the undoing of MG Refining & Marketing. Deutsche Bank's liquidity group published a glossy brochure, carrying the Deutsche Bank and Metallgesellschaft logos, in which it offered clients five-year and ten-year oil swaps with the fatal buy-out option. Clients could cash in any time that their swap went into the money. The brochure declared:

The cash-in price of the swap is based on the swap price. So the client knows at any time how much his swap position is worth. He can follow exactly how high his gain is, if the market had developed favourably. With the contractual guarantee of cancellation and objective methodology we provide total liquidity for the client, even for a ten-year oil swap.

This appears to be no different from the product marketed by MG Refining & Marketing in America, of which Schmitz himself was later so critical in an interview with *Euromoney*:

They [MG Refining & Marketing] wrote a type of contract which allowed in essence the client to run away from his obligations simply by shifting his commitment into a time along the time axis where the price-versus-hedge relationship is favourable to him. You can never book a receivable vis-à-vis this client if at the end of the day you never know whether you're going to have a receivable at all. These types of contracts account for about 60% of the portfolio and they were done roughly in one month. We're talking about a very big volume of exposure. 60% of this was done in the last month prior to the end of the fiscal year [September 30th 1993]. The objective was obvious – to prop up annual results. But the type of contract they used there had not been there before. So they invented a new contract – one that was out of any reasonable business logic – and forced these contracts down the throat of their clients. Why did the clients do that? Because this was an off-market deal, something that nobody offers, and, on the face of it, it looked very attractive.

Schmitz was the board member responsible for the liquidity group that chose to market a product that seems remarkably like the one he described above. Members of the liquidity group must have been well qualified to ask themselves how MG Corp was hedging what it offered. Did it not occur to them that, even at low volumes, MG Corp – unless it did identical back-to-back oil swaps with other clients and hence made no money – would have had to hedge this kind of product with near-month contracts on the New York Mercantile Exchange taking the rollover risk?

Deutsche Bank was careful to say in its brochure:

MG Refining & Marketing Inc is guaranteed by Metallgesellschaft AG as the counterparty in the business brokered by Deutsche Bank.

Under German banking law at the time, a German bank could not deal in commodities. Clients might have been forgiven, however, for assuming there was some kind of Deutsche Bank seal of approval. In the event, according to Deutsche Bank, there was no client interest in Germany and the marketing project was shelved.

15 Lessons from the collapse of Long-Term Capital Management

The collapse of Long-Term Capital Management, a giant hedge fund – along with the collapse of Barings, the Russian meltdown, and the trouble Metallgesellschaft and Procter & Gamble got into with their derivatives trading – are all events in the financial markets that provide lessons for the future. The common weakness in these cases was the misguided assumption that "our counterparty and the market it was operating in were performing within manageable limits". But once those limits were crossed, for whatever reason, disaster was difficult to head off.

The LTCM fiasco contains lessons about:

- model risk;
- unexpected correlation or the breakdown of historical correlations;
- the need for stress-testing;
- the value of disclosure and transparency;
- the danger of overgenerous extension of trading credit;
- the woes of investing in star quality; and
- investing too little in game theory – because LTCM's partners were playing a game up to the hilt.

John Meriwether, who founded LTCM in 1993, had been head of fixed-income trading at Salomon Brothers. Even when forced to leave Salomon in 1991, in the wake of the firm's treasury auction rigging scandal, Meriwether continued to command huge loyalty from a team of highly cerebral relative-value fixed-income traders and considerable respect from Wall Street.

With a team comprising a handful of these traders, Robert Merton and Myron Scholes (two Nobel laureates) and David Mullins (a former regulator), Meriwether and LTCM had more credibility than the average broker/dealer on Wall Street.

It was a game, in that LTCM was unregulated, was free to operate in any market without capital charges and had to make only rudimentary reports to the Securities and Exchange Commission (SEC). It traded on its good name with many respectable counterparties as if it was a member of the same club. This meant it was able to put on interest rate swaps at the market rate for no initial margin – an essential part of its strategy – and to borrow 100% of the value of any top-grade collateral, and with that cash to buy more securities and post them as collateral for further borrowing. In theory, it could leverage itself to infinity. In LTCM's first two full years of operation it produced 43% and 41% return on equity and had amassed an investment capital of $7 billion.

"Low-risk" arbitrage

Meriwether was a famous relative-value trader. Relative value means (in theory) taking little outright market risk, since a long position in one instrument is offset by a short position in a similar instrument or its derivative. It means betting on small price differences that are likely to converge over time as the arbitrage is spotted by the rest of the market and eroded. Typical trades in LTCM's early days were, for example, to buy Italian government bonds and sell German Bund futures; and to buy theoretically underpriced off-the-run American Treasury bonds (because they are less liquid) and run a short position in on-the-run (more liquid) treasuries. It played the same arbitrage in the interest-rate swap market, betting that the spread between swap rates and the most liquid Treasury bonds would narrow. It played long-dated callable Bunds against D-mark swaptions. It was one of the biggest players on the world's futures exchanges, not only in debt but also in equity products.

To make 40% return on capital, however, leverage had to be applied. In theory, market risk is not increased by stepping up volume, provided you stick to liquid instruments and do not get so big that you yourself become the market.

Some of the big macro hedge funds had encountered this problem and reduced their size by giving money back to their investors. When, in the last quarter of 1997, LTCM returned $2.7 billion to investors, it was assumed to be for the same reason: a prudent reduction in its positions relative to the market.

But it seems the positions were not reduced relative to the capital reduction, so the leverage increased. Moreover, other risks had been added to the equation. LTCM played the credit spread between mortgage-backed securities (including Danish mortgages) or AA corporate bonds and the government bond markets. Then it ventured into equity trades. It sold equity index options, taking a big premium in 1997. It took speculative positions in takeover stocks, according to press reports. One such was Tellabs, whose share price fell over 40% when it failed to take over Ciena, says one account. A filing with the SEC for June 30th 1998 showed that LTCM had equity stakes in 77 companies, worth $541m. It also got into emerging markets, including Russia. One report said Russia was "8% of its book", which would come to $10 billion.

Some of LTCM's biggest competitors, the investment banks, had been clamouring to buy into the fund. Meriwether applied a formula that brought in new investment, as well as providing him and his partners with a virtual put option on the performance of the fund. During 1997, under this formula (see page 150), UBS put in $800m in the form of a loan and $266m in straight equity. Credit Suisse Financial Products put in a $100m loan and $33m in equity. Other loans might have been secured in this way, but they have not been made public. Investors in LTCM were pledged to keep their money in for at least two years.

LTCM entered 1998 with its capital reduced to $4.8 billion.

According to a *New York Sunday Times* article by Michael Lewis,[10] the big trouble for LTCM started on July 17th when Salomon Smith Barney announced it was liquidating its dollar interest arbitrage positions:

> *For the rest of that month, the fund dropped about 10% because Salomon Brothers was selling all the things that Long-Term owned.*

On August 17th Russia declared a moratorium on its dollar-denominated domestic debt. Hot money, already jittery because of the Asian crisis, fled into high-quality instruments. The preference was for the most liquid American and rich-country government bonds. Spreads widened even between on-the-run and off-the-run American Treasury bonds.

Most of LTCM's bets had been variations on the same theme: convergence between liquid treasuries and more complex instruments that commanded a credit or liquidity premium. Unfortunately, convergence turned into dramatic divergence.

Calls for collateral

LTCM's counterparties, marking their LTCM exposure to market at least once a day, began to call for more collateral to cover the divergence. On one single day, August 21st, the LTCM portfolio lost $550m, wrote Lewis. Meriwether and his team, still convinced of the logic behind their trades, believed all they needed was more capital to see them through a distorted market.

Perhaps they were right. But several factors were against LTCM.

- Who could predict the timeframe within which rates would converge again?
- Counterparties had lost confidence in themselves and LTCM.
- Many counterparties had put on the same convergence trades, some of them as disciples of LTCM.
- Some counterparties saw an opportunity to trade against LTCM's known or imagined positions.

In these circumstances, leverage is not welcome. LTCM was being forced to liquidate to meet margin calls.

On September 2nd Meriwether sent a letter to his investors saying that the fund had lost $2.5 billion or 52% of its value that year, $2.1 billion in August alone. Its capital base had shrunk to $2.3 billion. Meriwether was looking for fresh investment of around $1.5 billion to carry the fund through. He approached those known to have such investible capital, including George Soros, Julian Robertson, Warren Buffett, chairman of Berkshire Hathaway and previously an investor in Salomon Brothers (LTCM, incidentally, had a $14m equity stake in Berkshire Hathaway), and Jon Corzine, then co-chairman and co-chief executive officer at Goldman Sachs, an erstwhile classmate at the University of Chicago. Goldman and J.P. Morgan were also asked to scour the market for capital.

But offers of new capital were not forthcoming. Perhaps these big players were waiting for the price of an equity stake in LTCM to fall further. Or perhaps they were making money just trading against LTCM's positions. In these circumstances, if true, it was difficult and dangerous for LTCM to show potential buyers more details of its portfolio. Two Merrill executives visited LTCM headquarters on September 9th for a "due diligence meeting", according to a later *Financial Times* report (on October 30th). They were provided with "general information about the fund's portfolio, its strategies, the losses to date and the intention to reduce risk". But LTCM did not disclose its trading positions, books or documents of any kind, Merrill is quoted as saying.

Ugly rumours

The US Federal Reserve system, particularly the New York Fed, which is closest to Wall Street, began to hear of concerns about LTCM from its constituent banks. In the third week of September, Bear Stearns, which was LTCM's clearing agent, said it wanted another $500m in collateral to continue clearing LTCM's trades. On Friday September 18th Bill McDonough, chairman of the New York Fed, made "a series of calls to senior Wall Street officials to discuss overall market conditions", he told the House Committee on Banking and Financial Services on October 1st.

> *Everyone I spoke to that day volunteered concern about the serious effect the deteriorating situation of Long-Term could have on world markets.*

Peter Fisher, executive vice-president at the New York Fed, decided to take a look at the LTCM portfolio. On Sunday September 20th he and two Fed colleagues, Gary Gensler, assistant treasury secretary, and bankers from Goldman and J.P. Morgan visited LTCM's offices at Greenwich, Connecticut. They were all surprised by what they saw. It was clear that although LTCM's major counterparties had closely monitored their bilateral positions, they had no inkling of LTCM's total off-balance-sheet leverage. LTCM had done swap upon swap with 36 different counterparties. In many cases it had put on a new swap to reverse a position rather than unwind the first swap, which would have required a mark-to-market cash payment in one direction or the other. LTCM's on-balance-sheet assets totalled around $125 billion on a capital base of $4 billion, a leverage of about 30 times. But that leverage was increased tenfold by LTCM's off-balance-sheet business, of which the notional principal ran to around $1 trillion.

The off-balance-sheet contracts were mostly nettable under bilateral ISDA (International Swaps and Derivatives Association) master agreements. Most of them were also collateralised. Unfortunately, the value of the collateral had taken a dive since August 17th.

Off the VaR scale

Surely LTCM, with two of the original masters of derivatives and option valuation among its partners, would have put its portfolio through stress-tests to match recent market turmoil. But like those of many other value-at-risk (VAR) modellers on Wall Street, their worst-case scenarios had been outplayed by the horribly correlated behaviour of the market since August 17th. Such a flight to quality had not been predicted, probably because it was so clearly irrational.

According to LTCM managers, their stress-tests had involved looking at the 12 biggest deals with each of their top 20 counterparties. This produced a worst-case loss of around $3 billion. But on that Sunday evening it seemed the mark-to-market loss, just on those 240 or so deals, might reach $5 billion. And this was ignoring all the other trades, some of them in highly speculative and illiquid instruments.

The next day, Monday September 21st, bankers from Merrill, Goldman and J.P. Morgan continued to review the problem. It was still hoped that a single buyer for the portfolio could be found, which would be the cleanest solution.

According to Lewis's article, LTCM's portfolio had its second biggest loss that day, of $500m. Half of that, says Lewis, was lost on a short position in five-year equity options. Lewis records brokers' opinion that American International Group (AIG) had intervened in thin markets to drive up the option price to profit from LTCM's weakness. At that time, as was learned later, AIG was part of a consortium negotiating to buy LTCM's portfolio. By this time LTCM's capital base had dwindled to a mere $600m. That evening, UBS, with its particular exposure on a $800m credit with $266m invested as a hedge, sent a team to Greenwich to study the portfolio.

Breakfast at the Fed

Fisher invited the three banks and UBS to breakfast at the Fed headquarters in Liberty Street the following day. The bankers decided to form working groups to study possible market solutions to the problem, given the absence of a single buyer. Proposals included buying LTCM's fixed-income positions and "lifting" the equity positions (which were a mixture of index-spread trades, total-return swaps and the takeover bets). During the day a third option emerged as the most promising: seeking recapitalisation of the portfolio by a consortium of creditors.

But any action had to be taken swiftly. The danger was that a single default by LTCM would trigger cross-default clauses in its ISDA master agreements, precipitating a mass close-out in the over-the-counter derivatives markets. Banks terminating their positions with LTCM would have to rebalance any hedge they might have on the other side. The market would quickly get wind of their need to rebalance and move against them. Mark-to-market values would descend in a vicious spiral. In the case of the CAC 40, the French equity index, LTCM had apparently sold short up to 30% of the volatility of the entire underlying market. The Banque de France was worried that a rapid close-out would severely hit French equities. There was a wider concern that an unknown number of market players had convergence positions similar or identical to those of LTCM. In such a one-way market, there could be a panic rush for the door.

A meltdown of developed markets on top of the panic in emerging markets seemed a real possibility. Bear Stearns was threatening to foreclose the next day if it did not see $500m more collateral. Until now, LTCM had resisted the temptation to draw on a $900m standby facility that had been syndicated by Chase Manhattan Bank, because it knew that the action would panic its counterparties. But the situation was now desperate. LTCM asked Chase for $500m. It received only $470m since two syndicate members refused to chip in.

To take the consortium plan further, the biggest banks, either big creditors of LTCM or big players in the over-the-counter markets, were asked to a meeting at the Fed that evening. The plan was to get 16 of them to chip in $250m each to recapitalise LTCM at $4 billion.

The four core banks met at 7pm and reviewed a term sheet drafted by Merrill Lynch. At 8.30pm bankers from nine more institutions showed up. They represented Bankers Trust, Barclays, Bear Stearns, Chase, Credit Suisse First Boston, Deutsche Bank, Lehman Brothers, Morgan Stanley, Crédit Agricole, Banque Paribas, Salomon Smith Barney and Société Générale. David Pflug, head of global credit risk at Chase, warned that nothing would be gained from raking over the mistakes that had got them into this room or arguing about who had the biggest exposure: they were all in this equally and together.

Damage limitation

The delicate question was how to preserve value in the LTCM portfolio, given that banks around the room would be equity investors and, at the same time, would be seeking to liquidate their own positions with LTCM to maximum advantage. It was clear that Meriwether and his partners would have to be involved in keeping such a complex portfolio a going concern. But what incentive would they have if they no longer had an interest in the profits? Chase insisted that any bail-out would first have to return the $470m drawn down on the syndicated standby facility. But nothing could be finalised that night since few of the representatives present could pledge $250m or more of their firm's money.

The meeting resumed at 9.30 the next morning. Goldman Sachs had a surprise: its client, Warren Buffett, was offering to buy the LTCM portfolio for $250m, and recapitalise it with $3 billion from his Berkshire Hathaway group, $700m from AIG and $300m from Goldman. There would be no management role for Meriwether and his team. None of LTCM's existing liabilities would be picked up, yet all current financing had to stay in place. Meriwether had until 12.30pm to decide.

By 1pm it was clear that Meriwether had rejected the offer, either because he did not like it, or, according to his lawyers, because he could not do so without consulting his investors, which would have taken him over the deadline.

The bankers were flabbergasted by Goldman's dual role. Despite frequent requests for information about other possible bidders, Goldman had dropped no hint at previous meetings that there was something in the pipeline. Now the banks were back to the consortium solution. Since there were only 13 banks, not 16, they would have to put in more than $250m each. Bear Stearns offered nothing, feeling that it had enough risk as LTCM's clearing agent. (Their special relationship may have been the source of some acrimony: LTCM had an $18m equity stake in Bear Stearns, matched by investments in LTCM of $10m each by Bear Stearns principals James Cayne and Warren Spector.) Lehman Brothers also declined to participate. In the end 11 banks put in $300m each, Société Générale $125m and Crédit Agricole and Paribas $100m each, reaching a total fresh equity of $3.625 billion. Meriwether and his team would retain a stake of 10% in the company. They would run the portfolio under the scrutiny of an oversight committee representing the new shareholding consortium.

Business as usual

The message to the market was that there would be no fire sale of assets. The LTCM portfolio would be managed as a going concern.

In the first two weeks after the bail-out LTCM continued to lose value, particularly on its dollar/yen trades, according to press reports, which put the loss at $200m–300m. There were more attempts to sell the portfolio to a single buyer. According to press reports the new LTCM shareholders had further talks with Buffett and with Alwaleed bin Talal bin Abdelaziz, a Saudi prince. But there was no sale. By mid-December the fund was reporting a profit of $400m, net of fees to LTCM partners and staff.

In early February 1999 there were press reports of divisions among the banks in the bail-out consortium, with some wishing to get their money out by the end of the year and others happy to "stay for the ride" of at least three years. There was also a dispute about how much Chase was charging for a funding facility to LTCM. Within six months there were reports that Meriwether and some of his team wanted to buy out the banks, with a little help from their friend Jon Corzine, who was to leave Goldman Sachs after its flotation in May.

By June 30th the fund was 14.1%, net of fees, higher than in the previous September. Meriwether's plan, approved by the consortium, was apparently to redeem the fund, now valued at around $4.7 billion, and to start another fund concentrating on buy-outs and mortgages. On July 6th LTCM repaid $300m to its original investors, who had a residual stake in the fund of around 9%. It also paid out $1 billion to the 14 consortium members. It seemed Meriwether had bounced back.

Post mortem

The LTCM fiasco naturally inspired a hunt for scapegoats.

- First in line were Meriwether and his crew of market professors.
- Second were the banks, which conspired to give LTCM far more credit, in aggregate, than they would have given a medium-size developing country. Particularly distasteful was the combination of credit exposure by the institutions themselves, and personal investment exposure by the individuals who ran them.

  Merrill Lynch protested that a $22m investment on behalf of its employees was not sinister. LTCM was one of four vehicles in which employees could opt to have their deferred payments invested. Nevertheless, this rather cosy relationship may have made it more difficult for credit officers to ask tough questions of LTCM. There were accusations of "croney capitalism" as Wall Street firms undertook to bail out, with shareholders' money, a firm in which their officers had invested, or were thought to have invested, part of their personal wealth.
- Third was the US Federal Reserve system. Although no public money was spent, apart from hosting the odd breakfast, there was the implication that the Fed was standing behind the banks, ready to provide liquidity until the markets became less jittery and more rational. Would this not simply encourage other hedge funds and lenders to hedge funds to be as reckless in future?
- Fourth was poor information. As with many hedge funds, scant disclosure of its activities and exposures was a major factor in

allowing LTCM to put on such leverage. There was also no mechanism whereby counterparties could learn how far LTCM was exposed to other counterparties.

- Fifth was sloppy market practice, such as allowing a non-bank counterparty to write swaps and pledge collateral for no initial margin as if it were part of a peer group of top-tier banks.

LTCM's risk management

Despite the presence of Nobel laureates closely identified with option theory, it seems LTCM relied too much on theoretical market-risk models and not enough on stress-testing, gap risk and liquidity risk. There was an assumption that the portfolio was sufficiently diversified across world markets to produce low correlation. But in most markets LTCM was replicating basically the same credit-spread trade. In August and September 1998 credit spreads widened in practically every market at the same time.

LTCM risk managers kidded themselves that the resultant net position of LTCM's derivatives transactions bore no relation to the billions of dollars of notional underlying instruments. Each of these instruments and its derivative has a market price that can shift independently, and each is subject to liquidity risk.

LTCM sources apparently complain that the market started trading against its known positions. This seems like special pleading. Meriwether *et al* must have been in the markets long enough to know they are merciless and to have been just as merciless themselves. "All they that take the sword shall perish with the sword."[11]

Risk management by LTCM counterparties

Practically everyone on Wall Street had a blind spot when it came to LTCM. They forgot the useful discipline of charging non-bank counterparties initial margin on swap and repo (stock borrowing) transactions. Collectively, they were responsible for allowing LTCM to build up layer upon layer of swap and repo positions.

They believed that the first-class collateral they held was sufficient to mitigate their loss if LTCM disappeared. It may have been over time, but their margin calls to top up deteriorating positions simply pushed LTCM further towards the brink. Their credit assessment of LTCM did not include a global view of its leverage and its relationship with other counterparties.

A working group on highly leveraged institutions set up by the Basel

Committee on Banking Supervision reported its findings in January 1999, drawing many lessons from the LTCM case. It criticised the banks for building up such exposures to such an opaque institution. They had placed a "heavy reliance on collateralisation of direct mark-to-market exposures", the report said.

> *This in turn made it possible for banks to compromise other critical elements of effective credit-risk management, including up-front due diligence, exposure measurement methodologies, the limit setting process, and ongoing monitoring of counterparty exposure, especially concentrations and leverage.*

The working group also noted that banks' covenants with LTCM "did not require the posting of, or increase in, initial margin as the risk profile of the counterparty changed, for instance as leverage increased". (For full reports see "Sound Practices for Banks' Interactions with Highly Leveraged Institutions" and "Banks' Interactions with Highly Leveraged Institutions", www.bis.org/bcbs.) Another report in June 1999 by the Counterparty Risk Management Policy Group, a group of 12 leading investment banks, suggested many ways in which information sharing and transparency could be improved. It noted the importance of measuring liquidity risk and improving market conventions and market practices, such as charging initial margin.

Supervision

Supervisors themselves demonstrated a certain blinkered view when it came to banks' and securities firms' relationships with hedge funds, and a huge fund like LTCM in particular. The SEC appeared to assess the risk run by individual broker/dealers, without having enough regard for what was happening in the sector as a whole, or in the firms' unregulated subsidiaries.

In testimony to the House Committee on Banking and Financial Services, on October 1st 1998, Richard Lindsey, director of the SEC's market regulation division, recalled the following:

> *When the commission learned of LTCM's financial difficulties in August, the commission staff and the New York Stock Exchange surveyed major broker/dealers known to have credit exposure to one or more large hedge funds. The results of our initial survey indicated that no individual broker/dealer had*

> *exposure to LTCM that jeopardised its required regulatory capital or its financial stability.*
>
> *As the situation at LTCM continued to deteriorate, we learned that although significant amounts of credit were extended to LTCM by US securities firms, this lending was on a secured basis, with collateral collected and marked-to-the-market daily. Thus, broker/dealers' lending to LTCM was done in a manner that was consistent with the firms' normal lending activity. The collateral collected from LTCM consisted primarily of highly liquid assets, such as US Treasury securities or G7 country sovereign debt. Any shortfalls in collateral were met by margin calls to LTCM. As of the date of the rescue plan, it appears that LTCM had met all of its margin calls by US securities firms. Moreover, our review of the risk assessment information submitted to the commission suggests that any exposure to LTCM existed outside the US broker/dealer, either in the holding company or its unregistered affiliates.*

The sad truth revealed by this testimony is that the SEC and the New York Stock Exchange were concerned only with the risk ratios of their registered firms and were ignorant and unconcerned, as were the firms themselves, about the market's aggregate exposure to LTCM.

Bank of England experts noted the absence of any covenant between LTCM and its counterparties that would have obliged LTCM to disclose its overall gearing. British banks had long been in the habit of demanding covenants from non-bank counterparties concerning their overall gearing, the Bank of England said.

Was there moral hazard?

The simple answer is yes, since the bail-out of LTCM gave comfort that the Fed will come in and broker a solution, even if it does not commit funds. Arguably, the Fed's intervention also tempted Meriwether not to accept the offer from Buffett, AIG and Goldman. The offer, heavily conditional though it was, shows that the LTCM portfolio had a perceived market value. A price might have been reached in negotiations between Buffett and Meriwether. Meriwether's (and the Fed's) argument is that Buffett's deadline of 12.30pm did not give Meriwether time to consult with LTCM's investors, so he was legally unable to accept the offer.

It is possible to argue that a market solution was found. Fourteen banks put up their own money, regarding it as a medium-term investment from which they expected to make a profit. From a value-preservation point of view it was an enlightened solution, even if it did seem to reward those whose recklessness had created the problem.

Alan Greenspan, chairman of the US Federal Reserve, defended its action at the October 1st hearing of the House Committee on Banking and Financial Services as follows:

> *This agreement [by the rescuing banks] was not a government bail-out, in that Federal Reserve funds were neither provided nor ever even suggested. Agreements were not forced upon unwilling market participants. Credits and counterparties calculated that LTCM and, accordingly, their claims, would be worth more over time if the liquidation of LTCM's portfolio was orderly as opposed to being subject to a fire sale. And with markets currently volatile and investors skittish, putting a special premium on the timely resolution of LTCM's problems seemed entirely appropriate as a matter of public policy.*

The true test of moral hazard is whether the Fed would be expected to intervene in the same way next time. Greenspan pointed to a unique set of circumstances that made a solution to LTCM's problems particularly pressing. It seems questionable whether the Fed would act as broker for another fund bail-out unless there were also such wide systemic uncertainties.

Was there truly a systemic risk?

Since there was no global meltdown, it is difficult to prove that there was a real danger of such a thing in September 1998. But if the officers at the Federal Reserve had waited to see what happened, no one would have thanked them after the event. The world financial system owes a lot to the prompt action of Greenspan, McDonough, Fisher and others at the Fed for their willingness to meet the problem fair and square. It is frightening to think what the Bank of England might have done, given its "constructive ambiguity" during the Barings crisis.

But the counter-argument is also valid. The Wall Street firms, once they knew the size of the problem, had only one sensible course of action: to bankroll a co-ordinated rescue. They had the resources to prevent a meltdown and it took only a night and a day to pool them. Mutual self-interest concentrates the mind wonderfully.

It seemed that in the developed world, since the early 1990s, financial firms had built up enough capital to meet most disasters the world could throw at them. Their mistakes in emerging markets were costly both for them and for the countries concerned, but they did not threaten the life of the world financial system. It seems the mechanisms for restructuring and acquisition were so swift that the demise of a financial firm simply meant it would be stripped of the trash and carved up. In a downward cycle, however, the outcome could be very different. Moreover, the social costs of this financial overreach, followed by cannibalism of assets, could be considerable.

Systemic? No. Ripe for concerted private and public intervention? Yes.

On September 29th 1998, six days after the LTCM bail-out, Greenspan cut Fed fund rates by 0.25% to 5.25%. On October 15th he cut them by another 0.25%. His critics associated these cuts directly with the bail-out of LTCM; it was an extra dose of medicine to make sure the recovery worked. Some sources attributed the cuts to rumours that another hedge fund was in trouble.

The more generous view is that if the financial markets were in disarray, worse might have come. Bruce Jacobs, who followed the systemic implications of the 1929, 1987 and subsequent mini-crashes, fearful of the dangers of globally traded derivatives, wrote:[12]

> *Had LTCM not been bailed out, the immediate liquidation of its highly leveraged bond, equity, and derivatives positions may have had effects, particularly on the bond market, rivalling the effects on the equity market of the forced liquidations of insured stocks in 1987 and margined stocks in 1929. Given the links between LTCM and investment and commercial banks, and between its positions in different asset markets and different countries' markets, the systemic risk much talked about in connection with the growth of derivatives markets may have become a reality.*

Corrective response

The Basel Committee on Banking Supervision's report on highly leveraged institutions (HLIs) in January 1999 suggested that supervisors should demand higher capital charges for exposure to highly leveraged institutions where there is no limit to overall leverage. "Possibly all exposures to all counterparties not covered by covenants on leverage should carry a higher weight." It further considered the possibility of extending a credit register for bank loans in the context of HLIs:

The register would entail collecting, in a centralised place, information on the exposures of international financial intermediaries to single counterparties that have the potential to create systemic risk [ie major HLIs]. Exposures would cover both on- and off-balance-sheet positions. Counterparties, supervisors and central banks could then obtain information about the overall indebtedness of the single counterparty.

The losers

Among the investors who lost their capital in LTCM (according to press reports) were:

- LTCM partners – $1.1 billion ($1.5 billion at the beginning of 1998, offset by its $400m stake in the rescued fund)
- UBS – $682m
- Dresdner Bank – $145m
- Bank of Italy – $100m
- Sumitomo Bank – $100m
- Credit Suisse – $55m
- Liechtenstein Global Trust – $30m
- Merrill Lynch (employees' deferred payment) – $22m
- Bear Stearns executives – $20m
- Donald Marron, chairman, PaineWebber – $10m
- McKinsey executives – $10m
- Sandy Weill, co-CEO, Citigroup – $10m
- Prudential Life Corp – $5.43m

There were no reported numbers for the following organisations:

- Bank Julius Baer (for clients)
- Republic National Bank
- St Johns University endowment fund
- University of Pittsburgh

UBS fiasco

The biggest single loser in the LTCM debacle was UBS, which was forced to write off Swfr950m ($682m) of its exposure. UBS's involvement with LTCM pre-dated the merger of Union Bank of Switzerland and Swiss Bank Corporation in December 1997. Various heads rolled, including that of Mathis Cabiallavetta, chairman (formerly chief executive of

UBS), Werner Bonadurer, chief operating officer, Felix Fischer, chief risk officer, and Andy Siciliano, head of fixed income (who had worked at SBC).

UBS's deal with LTCM was a variation on other attempts to turn hedge funds into a securitised asset class with protection against loss. However, in this case UBS was protecting against the loss and LTCM was taking a good deal of the gain. The sweetener for UBS was a structure that looked more like an option than a loan, turning any income into a capital gain, and an opportunity to invest directly in LTCM.

For a premium of $300m, UBS sold LTCM a seven-year European call option on 1m of LTCM's own shares, then valued at $800m. To hedge the position – the only way it could be done – UBS bought $800m worth of LTCM shares. UBS also invested $300m (most of the $266m premium income) directly in LTCM. Such an investment had to be held for a minimum of three years. This transaction was completed in three tranches in June, August and October 1997.

The deal was calculated so that the $300m premium was equivalent to a coupon of LIBOR plus 50 basis points over the seven years. Assuming that LTCM performed well, the deal provided UBS with steady, tax-efficient return plus a share in the upside, through its $266m stake. But if ever its hedge looked like falling below the $800m strike price, it was looking at a loss. The only way to hedge it would have been to sell LTCM shares.

But there were various impediments to this. UBS could not just dump the shares. It was obliged to convert any shares it sold into a loan at par value, maturing in 2004. Shares in hedge funds are not liquid, and LTCM's were no exception. It was impossible to mark them regularly to market. LTCM reported to shareholders only monthly. If UBS did sell LTCM shares in a falling market, and then LTCM's performance picked up again, there was no guarantee it could re-hedge its position. No one was making a market in LTCM shares.

Theoretically, there was a volatility cap on the arrangement. If the fund's volatility exceeded a certain level, a cash sum would be reckoned in UBS's favour, payable at the end of year seven. But it is not clear how this would have left UBS safely hedged.

Star-struck bankers

In the climate of mid-1997, it is understandable that UBS risk managers might have overlooked the horrible implications of a worst-case scenario. LTCM had a fantastic reputation for big-number but low-risk arbitrage. (There is a parallel in the reputation that Nick Leeson enjoyed at Barings before March 1995.) But it is clear now that UBS risk managers never faced the possibility of LTCM's collapse, which would have left them with $766m exposure ($800m hedge, $266m investment, less $300m option premium). That is, they did not wake up to it, apparently, until around April 1998, in a post-merger review, when it was too late to do much about it.

Credit Suisse Financial Products, which did a similar deal for $100m, set that as the maximum it was prepared to lose.

An interesting aspect of the UBS deal is to consider it from LTCM's point of view. LTCM secured $800m of new investment capital from UBS at a cost of 50 basis points above LIBOR per year. Once it had made enough return on its investment to cover these interest payments it could keep any further profits itself, and UBS had no further reward for the risk it was running. UBS's obligation to convert any shares that it wanted to sell into a loan to LTCM gave LTCM the equivalent of a put option on its own performance; that is, its insurance for bad performance was that UBS would become a lender to it rather than a shareholder. It was a cheap additional source of money to gamble with, with an insurance back-up if things went wrong. This was surely an added incentive for LTCM to roll the dice.

16 The crash of Mulhouse Brand

A financial crisis is not just about numbers that do not add up. It is about players and regulators who make up the market. You can stress-test numbers on a computer, but you cannot stress-test people, unless you pit them against each other in a simulation as close as possible to the real thing. They must be thrown into it suddenly, and be forced to make decisions on scanty information under severe time pressure. It must make them sweat.

With this objective, *Euromoney*, assisted by the London-based Centre for the Study of Financial Innovation (CSFI) and PA Consulting Group, invited 50 experienced financial experts, including active bankers and regulators, to throw themselves into an artificial but plausible crisis, set a year ahead in August 1998. Among the advisers who helped construct the simulation were bankers, senior regulators and the British army, which runs complex "Theatre of War" games for up to ten days each year.

Little concern for the system

The main lesson learned from this game was that when a global crisis looms, bankers and their regulators look after their self-interest first rather than co-operate for the common good. Short-term advantage is preferred, and long-term survival and the good of the system are neglected until it is nearly too late. It took most of a weekend, compressed into a few hours, for the British and American financial sectors to get their act together, whereas within ten minutes the Germans had formed a united front of banks and regulators and turned a financial crisis into an opportunity. Multilateral bodies such as the IMF and the Bank for International Settlements (BIS) found themselves powerless while time-horizons were so short and the priorities were so narrowly national.

In a simulation that was meant to show a way out of a global meltdown, without winners or losers, the surprise outcome was the fierce rivalry between financial centres. The American banks were still fighting yesterday's battles over assets already lost and blaming their regulators for being so weak, and the British banks and regulators were content with assuring themselves that it was "not their problem". The simulation ended in an apparent victory for the Germans and their well-known consensus system.

This is all seen with the benefit of hindsight. In the heat of battle, with limited information spread asymmetrically among the players, the landscape looked very different. The German banks and regulators were suspected of resorting to a little pre-game collusion, which shows how badly they wanted to win.

Crisis building

The crisis begins with an earthquake in California on August 10th 1998. Elmas, a Miami-based boutique trading Latin American debt and equity, finds itself caught with positions in Californian earthquake bonds worth close to zero, and looming losses related to the hedge that it constructed – selling call options on the level of a regional property index – which perversely goes up not down. At this stage, no one – except Alberto Schultz, Elmas's maverick CEO/president – knows how many options Elmas has sold and to whom, but the losses could be several billion dollars.

Simple enough to contain, you might think. Elmas goes bust and its creditors and counterparties lose their money.

But there are complications. Elmas is owned by Mulhouse Brand & Co (MBC), a once venerable British merchant bank. MBC was bought in 1992 by Federated Scottish Banks (FSB), a British clearing bank, which in early 1998 sold a majority stake in MBC to Bayerische Kreditbank (BKB), Germany's fifth-biggest bank. With 65% of MBC, BKB would appear to be the merchant bank's ultimate parent and lender of last resort. But since the ink on the sale is hardly dry, the Bavarians have an excuse not to take responsibility.

Apart from these three fictitious banks, each represented by actors playing the chairman, the treasurer and legal counsel, all other institutions in the drama have real names. Financial experts turned actor play Alan Greenspan, chairman of the US Federal Reserve, Hans Tietmeyer, president of the Bundesbank, Eddie George, governor of the Bank of England, Howard Davies, head of the Securities and Investments Board (the SIB was the immediate forerunner of the Financial Services Authority), Michel Camdessus, head of the IMF, Andrew Crockett, head of the BIS, and a galaxy of senior bankers, including Rolf Breuer and Jürgen Sarrazin, heads of Deutsche Bank and Dresdner Bank, Sir William Purves, chairman of HSBC, and Dick Fisher and Frank Newman, heads of Morgan Stanley and Bankers Trust. There is also a press corps, acting as vital disseminators of information, disinformation, intelligent guesswork and propaganda (see full list of players, page 173).

The ten interest groups have private rooms linked by telephone. They can arrange meetings, use the press to spread stories and negotiate one-to-one in the corridors or in two "safe" houses: the Monte Carlo room and the Savoy Suite. There is an auditorium for plenary sessions and a press club for refreshment and gossip, where there is the risk of being wrong-footed by a journalist.

Each participant has an information pack containing publicly known information and a personal information sheet containing facts – sometimes accurate, sometimes misleading – known only to him or her. As in the army games, there are an exercise director, a college of arbitrators and controllers providing market information and other guidance as required.

Prelude to the action

It is a hot Thursday night in August. Howard Davies, head of the SIB, Britain's new super financial regulator, is watching his favourite video – Manchester City football team beating the hell out of arch-rivals Manchester United back in 1989 – when the telephone rings.

It is Sir Roy McTaggart, chairman of FSB. He sounds angry and confused, railing against spivs in the City of London and their ungovernable greed. "I think you should call Birkenhead for an explanation. He'll need a good one."

Davies calls Lord Birkenhead, chairman of MBC.

"Do you have a problem you want to discuss?" Davies asks Birkenhead.

"Nothing we can't handle."

Davies is not impressed. "I want you and your chief financial officer at the SIB within 20 minutes."

Birkenhead and his chief financial officer, Peter Butter, arrive at the SIB; so do Davies and his head of supervision, Michael Foot.

"It's nothing we can't handle," repeats Birkenhead. "We've had some rather heavy calls for collateral in America, and we're having to scrabble around for cash."

"What about FSB? Can't it take up the slack?"

"McTaggart says we're no longer his problem."

"What about your Bavarian friends?" asks Davies.

"They don't see us as their responsibility yet." (The sale of 65% of MBC has just gone through.)

"Right," asks Davies. "What is the shortfall?"

Birkenhead and Butter look at each other. "It keeps changing. At the last count it was about $2 billion."

"And how much have you raised so far?"

"Nearly $750m," says Butter. "But America is still open and we've got our interbank traders on the job."

This is how British regulators learn about a crisis brewing at MBC. But the market has already smelled trouble for MBC's parents, FSB and BKB. It began when an earthquake hit California four days earlier, on Monday August 10th.

The two big banks are now experiencing funding difficulties in the interbank market. BKB faces a rating downgrade to single A, because of its portfolio of bad east German loans and the cost of the MBC acquisition. There are also reports that BKB is no longer considered by most banks as an acceptable swap counterparty.

What does the market know that the regulators do not? Elmas, a Miami-based financial boutique, has been over-extending itself. It has arranged $3.2 billion part-collateralised project financing in Brazil; it has been joint underwriter of a $5 billion bond issue for the California Earthquake Authority, keeping $1.5 billion in its trading portfolio; and it has written over-the-counter call options on a California property index that looks extremely volatile.

Monday's earthquake has all but wiped out the principal of the California earthquake bonds, which are designed to lose value if an earthquake hits, as a form of reinsurance for the earthquake authority. The calls on the property index, designed to hedge the earthquake bonds, could be exercised at any time, because the index has capriciously soared instead of falling. This is because it is based on earthquake-proof buildings, whose value has gone up since the earthquake. Elmas, facing margin calls from its counterparties, has to raise cash fast.

It tries to re-pledge the collateral from its Brazilian project financing, but finds its title to the securities is imperfect and the project has turned sour; the maximum possible loss is $3.2 billion. Moreover, its main creditor in Brazil, Banco Terror, is calling in the entire sum on the strength of a letter of credit provided by MBC, which has owned Elmas since 1994.

Enough people in the market make the connection between Elmas, via MBC, to MBC's 35% parent, FSB, and its 65% parent, BKB. Major banks quietly reduce credit lines and drive up the big banks' funding costs.

The game begins

From this point, the action is compressed into six hours representing three-and-a-half days, from Friday morning until Monday noon. The pressure on decision-making is considerable. Perhaps there could be many outcomes, but below is an account of what happened, pieced together from the participants' notebooks, tape recorders in each room (but sometimes they were switched off) and debriefing sessions. Remember that the personalities below were represented in a simulation and their actions in no way represent the real-life actions of the named officials.

Day 1, Friday August 14th 1998

0800 The Bank of England and the SIB demand to see MBC's books. The piece of paper that prevents MBC from letting Elmas go bust is an irrevocable letter of credit for $3.2 billion which Butter, MBC's finance director, rashly signed without board approval only weeks ago to keep Elmas's creditors off its back. Schultz, president of Elmas, used the letter of credit to back $3.2 billion of credit from Banco Terror.

Legal opinion suggests this guarantee from the finance director, even without board approval, cannot be wriggled out of. MBC, in honouring the guarantee, will see its $1.3 billion capital wiped out. Schultz also appears to have used MBC guarantees to back Elmas's option positions. Within minutes of opening for business on Friday, MBC receives calls from Morgan Stanley, Bankers Trust and others demanding to exercise their property options and, in the event of non-payment by Elmas, seeking recourse from the guarantor, MBC.

0830 Birkenhead, chairman of MBC, manages to stall these demands, promising to have the position clarified by Monday. "If you can just bear with me for a little while I'm sure we'll be able to settle this matter fairly promptly," Birkenhead tells Fisher, chairman of Morgan Stanley.

Birkenhead calls McTaggart, head of FSB, hoping he can provide funding for the weekend. But the Scottish bank refuses to give explicit support.

Meanwhile, in Munich, the board of BKB is asking: "Do we own the thing?" Was there any written commitment to support MBC, and "what would be the damage to our reputation if we let it go down?". BKB gets a call from McTaggart suggesting a meeting, and another call from Wolfgang Artopoeus, its chief supervisor, in Berlin. At the same time Sabine Schröder, a *Finanzblatt* journalist, tries to gatecrash the meeting and is kicked out. She is following up a press report from Miami that BKB also bought earthquake bonds from Elmas and is now sitting on a loss of $2.5 billion. Eugen Toplitz, chairman of BKB, fiercely denies this, only to be told quietly by Hannes Ross, his treasurer, that it is partly true. Ross bought $1.5 billion of the bonds from Schultz, but now blames the purchase on one of his traders who was "acting outside his authority".

The Bundesbank and three big German banks – Deutsche, Dresdner and Westdeutsche Landesbank – not knowing the size of the problem but seeing a threat to Finanzplatz Deutschland, act promptly. After a ten-minute meeting they decide to stand behind BKB. The German banks provide a $1 billion loan collateralised with BKB's estimated $900m worth of industrial holdings. But to solve the wider problem, the Bundesbank needs commitment from the Bank of England and a British bank consortium to stand behind FSB and MBC. "I'm not putting in a *pfennig* to save Mulhouse Brand," says Tietmeyer, president of the Bundesbank. He regards the Elmas fiasco as a British problem.

0900 Dresdner Bank in the meantime plays a maverick game, selling Dax futures in case the German stockmarket tumbles, and buying put options on the shares of FSB. We learn why later.

The American banks – Bank of America, Bankers Trust and Morgan Stanley – are most concerned about their in-the-money options positions with Elmas and whether they will get paid today's value of roughly $700m between them. It seems unlikely. They want their regulators to get tough with the British and the Germans, but Greenspan seems to be tied up in meetings. Bankers Trust, in the meantime, is trying to liquidate its swap positions with BKB, where it has net positive value of $125m.

1100 The Bank of England and the British banks – Barclays, HSBC and SBC Warburg – agree to keep FSB afloat in the interbank market, at least until the end of the day. But they will not stand behind MBC.

1400 As the American markets are about to open, the British regulators give a press conference, saying that British clearers have offered support to stabilise the situation but are not writing a blank cheque. Davies says he is setting up a 24-hour control room and information centre, but this is the last we hear of it.

German largesse

1430 Soon afterwards the Bundesbank issues a statement saying it is willing to inject sufficient funds into the German system to maintain liquidity. Tietmeyer says he is "in discussion" with American officials. Greenspan says there is "no cause for alarm". But he has domestic concerns in the aftermath of the earthquake and the overheating of the American economy. A rise in interest rates is predicted.

Nobody knows the extent of the property index losses, and there are worries about a banking crisis in Brazil and the soundness of collateralisation there. Banco Terror's $3.2 billion hole could trigger a run on itself and other Brazilian banks, as creditors race to realise their assets. There is a fear that private deals are being cut in the corridors of power. The temptation is to look after yourself and forget about the others.

1600 Hans de Gier, chief executive of SBC Warburg, reflects as he and the other British banks are kept waiting for a meeting with the Bank of England: "The Bank of England has obviously panicked. As we leave the meeting we hear rumours of much larger losses. We are surprised to find press reports from the Bank guaranteeing liquidity. We haven't guaranteed anything. I'm stalling the American banks until I have up-to-date information."

The IMF, the BIS and the European Central Bank (ECB) are having trouble persuading the players to come to terms with the size of the problem – they think this is the tip of the iceberg. They cannot get clear figures out of the Bank of England or the Germans.

Crockett opines: "The smaller British banks could have trouble renewing their lines if a major liquidity crisis flares up. The problem is the sheer weight of money, primarily the huge derivative transactions that are around, and the great fear is that there will be a crisis when the clearing system just breaks down. A possible solution would be a bank holiday."

Vanishing villain

1640 Schultz, on his yacht in Miami, gives a press conference and confirms that he sold BKB $1.5 billion of earthquake bonds, which are now at 5% of par. He denies that his activities involve money laundering.

Jim Herzog, acting head of the Commodities and Futures Trading Commission (CFTC), moves to get Schultz arrested ("I want him naked, homeless and without wheels"). But Schultz has planned his exit and is on a plane to Mexico.

1715 Meanwhile, the audit team trawling through the Elmas office in Miami find tickets suggesting the property index position could total $3 billion or higher if the options are exercised at today's price. American regulators hear a rumour that the property index in California is being manipulated.

Then it appears that the foreign-exchange market is under threat. MBC's office in New York reports that it is still waiting for a $200m payment through Chips as part of a spot transaction against Indonesian rupiah which it delivered to Ravi Asian Bank in Jakarta. "If it doesn't arrive by the time Chips closes, at 6pm EST," says MBC, "we will have a liquidity problem. Can you forward sufficient funds to cover?"

FSB, approached for liquidity, says it might support if BKB supports, but it has to know the full extent of the problem.

Crockett advises that all three banks should be liquidated now and the Brazilian aspect should be addressed. "My instinct tells me that the parents are insolvent – I have seen too many bust banks before. The BIS is concerned that there is a major international liquidity crisis building up and we have people from different countries in different places trying to manage the crisis in an independent way. The situation is already bigger than just these banks." But his advice goes unheeded.

1800 Confidence in the trio of banks is not helped by a spurious story from Doug Deeply of the *Daily Stun*:

> *It has been claimed that the motive behind the acquisition of Mulhouse Brand was so that Eugen Toplitz, a senior official at Bayerische Kreditbank, could be near his mistress in Palm Springs. He spent time at wild fancy dress parties, dressing up in uniform. "You should have concentrated on the bank's business, Topless!"*

Bankers' slow reactions

1830 Camdessus at the IMF writes in his diary: "It's hard to avoid the conclusion that these events need to be handled by beginning with some worst-case planning in order to close down those worst-case possibilities, then work backwards. The banks appear to be working out from the specific problem, so they're always behind the eight-ball [too slow in their reactions]." Camdessus expresses "considerable concern that the Americans are now privately saying to the IMF that they are unhappy with the British response".

At the ECB, Wim Duisenberg agrees: "Lack of clarity on the size of the problem is the main difficulty. Our feeling is that central banks are overoptimistic in assessing the problem."

1900 The Bundesbank tells Davies and George that it is ensuring the liquidity of BKB with a $1 billion Lombard facility, $1.5 billion in loans from the big German banks, against BKB's industrial shareholdings, and an undertaking to stand behind any swaps that need to be reassigned because of BKB's imminent credit downgrade, up to $10 billion in nominal principal.

But this leaves open the question of who takes responsibility for Elmas and MBC, and ignores the effect on American creditors and banks in Brazil. In America the Dow Jones Industrial Average falls 200 points in early afternoon trading. The stocks most heavily affected are banks, insurance companies and major California-based firms.

1930 The British banks and regulators are preoccupied with their own backyard, wondering whether to rescue FSB. De Gier writes: "The SBC position is to let MBC go. My only interest in FSB is participating in a Bank of England-led rescue. Do we keep it afloat?"

"Yes," says Martin Taylor, chief executive of Barclays, "so long as we don't pick up the American and German element. We don't want to let another British bank go down, but we need to establish a *cordon sanitaire.*"

2100 The American banks continue to call Schultz, Elmas and MBC in an attempt to exercise their options and close out their swap positions. Schultz, when reached by telephone, refers callers to MBC. MBC can only keep up its stalling tactics, hoping that a solution will be found by Monday.

2200 The BKB board, sitting late into Friday night, is split down the middle. Ross insists that MBC must be cut loose and allowed to sink, regardless of the effect on the Bavarian bank's reputation. "We're talking about survival." Actually he's talking about his own survival, since any other solution is likely to reveal that he was behind the unauthorised purchase of earthquake bonds. "If we sell our shares in FSB (FSB and BKB already have 4.9% cross-shareholdings in each other) it makes it easier to walk away from MBC," says Ross. "We're going to pull the plug on MBC, so forget any friendship with FSB."

Toplitz and Michaela Funk, a board member, would like to do the honourable thing: bail out MBC and pre-empt the argument with FSB by taking it over. "If they're not getting support from the market," says Funk, "why don't we buy FSB for a pound?" Merging with FSB would continue BKB's Europe-wide expansion in the mortgage business.

Anglo-German spat

2300 As midnight approaches, the temperature is rising between the British and German regulators. At an informal bilateral meeting a Bundesbanker exclaims: "It's no surprise the regulators of Barings don't know what's happening." A Bundesbank source feeds the press a line: "The British authorities will tomorrow face an ultimatum from the German authorities. We believe it's time for them to stop the rot over there as we have done over here."

2400 The failed foreign-exchange deal in east Asia, apparently ignored in the heat of squabbles nearer home, hangs over the proceedings like a sword of Damocles. In the small hours of the morning an e-mail appears on the screens of all subscribers to the Swift system:

> *The holy man at Ravi Asian Bank has been sent by god to purge and cleanse the world financial system. His act of denial should be followed by others. Only after the expectoration and destruction of all complex financial instruments can international trade and foreign relations continue in the course of truth and light.*

Day 2, Saturday August 15th 1998

0800 Executives of FSB and BKB meet to try to co-ordinate a rescue of MBC, but perhaps they are only going through the motions. Neither side is aware that MBC gave Elmas a $3.2 billion letter of credit, which is lost. Both sides protest that they have no direct exposure to MBC apart from the equity. In an atmosphere of tension and aggression, the Palm Springs story comes up again. "You started the mud-slinging," says BKB. BKB receives the unpleasant news that Vaclav Bank, its subsidiary in the Czech Republic, is in trouble with bad loans and a funding problem. It needs a cash injection. FSB learns that its branches in Mexico City and São Paulo have had similar problems.

0820 In the eye of the storm, things do not look good either. An irate Birkenhead at MBC refers press enquiries "to our parent BKB". "Is BKB your parent?" asks a reporter bravely before being thrown out. The beleaguered MBC board discusses what to do next. "Should we make a bland statement? I know we should speak through BKB but relations with them are strained. We have until Monday to sort this out. When the East Asian markets open we will be dead and buried." Wendy Nelson, an in-house lawyer, sees the American banks as the biggest danger to the bank's survival: "We have one and a half days to force the American regulators to make the American banks back off and we have to get the British and the Germans to rescue us." Nelson suggests they "just deny anything other than the $3.2 billion".

0935 The American banks feel relatively secure. They are not likely to be made insolvent, but they want to get paid. A press report from Asia does not seem to ruffle them; perhaps they're suffering from information overload:

> *Reuters, Jakarta: Hugo Chew, chairman of Ravi Asian Bank, is unrepentant about his refusal to honour a $200m spot foreign-exchange deal with a British merchant bank. The act may precipitate a worldwide payments crisis, say experts. "I have my own shareholders to think of," says Chew. Chew says there is no certainty that Mulhouse Brand will be open for business on Monday. Ravi Asian has $350m in medium-term deposits with Mulhouse Brand, and funds with its asset management arm, which it wishes to safeguard, Chew says.*

Camdessus reflects: "We need to put something in place to make sure that foreign-exchange markets open and behave in the normal way. There may need to be a statement at G7 [a summit meeting of leading industrial countries starting that day in Britain] about determination of world financial markets to withstand crisis, especially given the press leaks."

Systemic alarm-bells

American, British and German regulators, meeting at Leeds Castle in Britain, discuss Brazil and the possible liquidity crisis there. "The losers are American or Brazilian," says Camdessus. "For us to live with Elmas going down, we need to know the implications for Brazil and America."

Crockett is concerned about a systemic crisis. "We need to know what other commitments apart from that to Brazil we need to give. It may be necessary to let Brazil go in order to save the US and Germany. We are not aware of the spill-through. The American banks may well be holding back the seriousness of the situation – they have a number of issues of their own and seem to be reluctant to involve international arbitration. Our concern must be total financial meltdown with companies failing one after the other." Duisenberg in a private note complains that he has "no power". "My only interest is to see that inflation in the euro zone to come doesn't rise above 2.5%. So I'm only giving advice when asked."

1000 At the crack of dawn American time the CFTC and the Securities and Exchange Commission announce they have put in officials to run Elmas, to protect investors' interests and gather information on its (potentially) fraudulent activities. Schultz has been lured to Washington for an interview with the CFTC. Afterwards he is arrested and refused bail. He is sent to a federal holding facility in Maryland.

1030 "We're going off to shoot grouse," Reuters reports Taylor as saying, "because we [the top British banks] see this crisis as a German problem." MBC board members also appear to have left their offices. The telephone is answered by the cleaning lady.

Good bank/bad bank

1100 Meanwhile, a consortium of big German banks swings into action to sort out the BKB problem. It says it has secured a good bank/bad bank split, putting BKB's bad east German loans and the equity stake in MBC and other related entities into Schlechte Bank, and its good assets into Neue-BKB. Neue-BKB has a positive net worth in excess of $3.5 billion, their press release says.

BKB seems unaware of this decision and is negotiating with FSB to buy its 35% stake in MBC "for one pound". Moreover, far from the grouse moor, Purves, chairman of HSBC, is discussing a private deal with Toplitz, possibly the sale of his bank to HSBC.

Purves is furious an hour later when he hears of the German bank consortium's plans for BKB: "So much for the Germans!" he thunders. The rumour mills continue to turn. The latest is that Bankers Trust is trying to buy MBC.

1400 By Saturday afternoon, notes Birkenhead, MBC is "totally marginalised. We've taken the phone off the hook". A press spokesperson for MBC says the directors are "out shooting grouse".

As they are leaving, a communication arrives from the audit team in Miami. They now have a near-complete account of the index options.

Holder	*No. of options ('000)*	*Value ($m)*
Bankers Trust	400	199
Bank of America	600	299
Morgan Stanley	400	199
CSFP	800	398
LTCM	2,000	996
Lazy z Property	2,000	996
Dry Gulch Estates	1,500	747
e-mail address inc	500	249
Savills	500	249
MEPC	500	249
Yokohama Land	1,500	747
Others (unrecorded)	3,900	1,942
Total	14,600	7,271

MBC's total known exposure to Elmas is now around $12 billion ($3.2 billion to Banco Terror, $1.5 billion in worthless earthquake bonds pledged to various parties and $7.3 billion in potential options losses).

A dubious property index

1600 Greenspan is trying to attack the American exposure at its root: the property index. "We have potentially $12 billion exposed – $7 billion for sure. Our objective is to get the index back down, preferably to nil. We can sustain up to $1.5 billion without affecting the taxpayer. We should guarantee the excess and then cook the market. If we declare a federal disaster, plough in insurance and bring up the non-earthquake-proof properties, that would reduce the value of the earthquake-proof properties and bring the value of the index down. We could claim we're concerned about the way the index is constructed. We could just declare the whole thing void and contrary to public policy. We would only hit speculators, hedge funds and banks, and they only lose paper profits. We should say to American banks: 'You support Elmas or we will declare it invalid. If you don't support Elmas we will declare a disaster and you can take your chances from that.'"

1700 At the G7 regulators' meeting at Leeds Castle the Bundesbank asks for support from Britain. But the British regulators' view is: "We'd be happy for MBC to go under."

1900 MBC's reaction is predictable: "We are stuffed and the last to know." Nelson complains: "I had hoped we would have been able to talk to the three of them before this happened. We are just powerless in Badco [Schlechte Bank]. Have we missed a trick by not contacting the American regulators?"

The American banks are also annoyed that the initiative has been seized by the Germans, who seem to be ignoring American banks' claims. "This is turning into one of those European messes," says Newman, head of Bankers Trust, "where everyone blames everyone else and it drags on for years and years. No one is prepared to step up for MBC who are on the hook to us." Adds Morgan Stanley's Fisher: "I can only assume the regulators don't believe there's really such a crisis."

Newman: "It's a crisis for us as business people, as bankers, and our ability to continue to be a viable concern. Will you trade with German banks on Monday, knowing what they've done to get out of this situation, and with the implicit backing of the central bank? One option is that on Monday we close our window to German banks and short the D-mark."

2130 Gustavo Franco, governor of Brazil's central bank, warns that 12 foreign bank subsidiaries in Brazil are exposed to Elmas and would not survive a crisis that threatens to become systemic.

2300 As day two comes to a close, two press reports suggest a mixed response even in Germany to the German banks' rescue package.

> *Finanzblatt: Allianz Versicherung, the largest investor in Europe and a major shareholder in BKB, has taken the unprecedented step of criticising openly a bank's strategy. Chairman Henning Schulte-Noelle said: "The half-baked plan cooked up by Deutsche Bank lacks substance and will not assuage the markets' fears come Monday." Bayerische Kreditbank will not comment, but Deutsche Bank speaker Rolf Breuer says: "Any criticism of this plan is implicitly a criticism of the Bundesbank."*
>
> *Reuters, Berlin: Jürgen Stark, secretary of state at the German finance ministry, has said that the British and American authorities are in full support of the rescue package for Bayerische Kreditbank put together by German commercial banks. Limited central bank funds were required.*

Day 3, Sunday August 16th 1998

0800 There is a meeting of creditors and multilateral institutions to discuss Brazil. The British banks have decided that the systemic risk in Brazil is the biggest problem. They volunteer a package of $1.5 billion (roughly $100m each from 12 banks) for six months. The IMF offers to match this amount with a three-month, $1.5 billion facility. The German banks have another agenda, which is to buy 49% of Banco Terror, the bank at the centre of the Brazilian crisis. They invite the governor of the Brazilian central bank for further talks.

The American regulators are considering forcing their banks to compromise on the property options. "We can put together a deal in which the American banks will lose some profit from the options, but they will not lose very much," says Greenspan. Later that day, as part of the plan, the American government pledges $100 billion in disaster relief for the Californian earthquake. They also discuss getting tougher with the British: "We could say that MBC and FSB will never be able to do business in America unless they support Elmas," says Greenspan. "We must be careful because there is some American bank exposure to BKB."

1200 The British banks are increasingly disillusioned by the Bank of England's lack of leadership. "Off the record," De Gier tells a journalist, "this crisis has shown the Bank of England to be a total lame duck. Far from being the lender of last resort, it has seemingly acquiesced in the rescue of a marginal bank by a German lifeboat, and we urgently seek clarification from the chancellor of the exchequer. Is it for the German banks to judge which institutions in Britain will affect our financial stability? I am deeply worried. We at SBC Warburg have interests as to whether London remains a financial centre." At this point there is a rumour that George, the Bank of England governor, has gone missing.

Eyes turn to Asia

1315 But George is trying to stave off what he sees as the bigger crisis: the failed spot foreign-exchange trade in east Asia. He calls the head of the Indonesian central bank who says he has told Chew at Ravi Asian that his bank may never deal in the foreign-exchange markets again, but he sympathises with Chew. Assurances must be given that the British bank MBC will be open for business on Monday morning. George cannot give such an assurance, but warns the Indonesian official: "$200m is small, but the market could seize up if everyone seeks set-off."

Meanwhile, McTaggart has a nasty surprise. FSB's auditor, Charibdis & Skiller, sends a note:

> *We have to express extreme concern that you seem to have withheld our original due-diligence report regarding potential exposures of Elmas and the lack of adequate control. We have to inform you that without an immediate indemnity we will be obliged to advise the* SIB *by 12 noon today.*

McTaggart warns Spiros Charibdis, a senior partner: "If you go public on this you're opening yourselves up to a charge of negligence." He asks who has seen the report and who signed it. Charibdis says FSB signed copies, and copies also went to BKB as part of the due diligence before the sale of 65% of MBC. "We at C&S passed comment on the lack of control and the potential exposure levels of Elmas," says Charibdis.

Iain Stewart, the treasurer, retorts: "You didn't brief the board at the time."

Charibdis: "I'm not suggesting any impropriety."

McTaggart: "Then what has changed?"

Stewart: "You say you raised these concerns within the bank. If they were major you should have brought them to the board."

Stewart calls Davies at the SIB. He points out that the auditors had not acted forcefully enough to prompt FSB to go to the authorities at the time.

Transatlantic ire

1350 *New York Times*: "American Banks Threaten Local Action".

In a joint press statement Bankers Trust, Morgan Stanley and Bank of America attacked European regulators for not getting to grips with the Elmas/MBC crisis and threatened to take further action if this remains unchanged. "We consider the MBC crisis to be a German issue, and the American banks will be looking to the German authorities, the German regulators and the German banks to resolve it. If they do not, the American banks will be forced to reconsider their position." This would probably take the form of seriously curtailing interbank dealing and other business with Germany.

The British regulators are belatedly trying to get FSB and a consortium of British banks to support MBC. But the British banks are adamant that they will only support FSB and that it should not use any of that support to bail out MBC.

1600 From America comes another potentially embarrassing report concerning FSB saying that Stewart, its treasurer, signed a comfort letter for some American banks 18 months ago, although the document is undated.

1630 The British banks tell George at the Bank of England that they will stop funding FSB and expel it from the Chaps clearing system unless the letter of comfort issue is resolved. FSB protests to George that the real issue is whether the sale of the controlling interest in MBC has been completed.

Tietmeyer demands a conference call with George and Davies. He presents them with some new information. The German banks believe FSB is bust, and they hold put options worth more than its equity. Dresdner Bank bought put options on Friday that are now $2.2 billion in the money. The German banks want to force FSB to rescue MBC with the backing of the Bank of England. "We German regulators are sick and tired of being viewed as the problem. You [the British] are the problem."

1830 The German banking consortium has pulled off a coup in Brazil: the purchase of 49% of Banco Terror. The Brazilian central bank governor apparently approved the sale after intensive discussions on a luxury yacht. Moreover, despite its alleged split into good bank/bad bank, BKB is negotiating to buy back its 4.9% stake in FSB.

Greenspan steps in

1945 MBC calls a press conference at which Birkenhead argues: "We have no legal or moral obligation to cover losses beyond MBC's $3.2 billion letter of credit. As far as we're concerned, it's a problem for the American authorities which regulate Elmas, and for American investors who took positions."

But the American regulators and banks are at sixes and sevens. Greenspan warns: "When the market opens tomorrow the property index will probably go down. You will lose some money."

American bank: "We need to know if we have a deal or not before the markets open. We want the Germans to make good on Elmas."

Greenspan: "What leverage do we have on the Germans?"

American bank: "We are American. This is what we're telling them they have to do."

Greenspan: "When the market opens you may find that the property index position goes from $7 billion to $3.5 billion in liabilities, so we will be down to $3.2 billion on the Germans."

American bank: "We are willing to take the hit if the market value of these options goes down, but not if they decide that they can't pay and won't pay."

Greenspan: "We're prepared to support the American banks on this line."

American bank: "Unless we have an agreement we're shorting the D-mark with everything we have tomorrow."

Greenspan: "We'd better let them know that."

The CFTC calls for calm and co-operation: "We shouldn't make any threats but say everyone should support each other."

2230 As Sunday night ends and the markets in Tokyo prepare to open, there is another German bombshell:

> *Finanzblatt: Germany's big banks have attempted to end the crisis of confidence in BKB by investing massive sums in the German equity market and in acquiring control of FSB. As the market opens, Finanzblatt can reveal exclusively that a consortium headed by Deutsche, Dresdner and WestLB has purchased $6 billion of Dax futures to boost confidence in the German equity market. In addition, the consortium has effectively acquired control of FSB by exercising 200m put options that it purchased at the beginning of the crisis at "extremely competitive" rates which are now worth some $2.5 billion. Eugen Toplitz, who evidently still enjoys the confidence of German banks, is CEO-designate of FSB.*

But neither the German nor the British authorities will confirm this, says Reuters, and it is "strongly denied" by McTaggart.

George immediately calls the German banks about the *Finanzblatt* story. They confirm that they hold the options. George says that provided they do not sell them he will consider a German takeover of FSB.

George calls Stewart at FSB: "The German banks inform me that at the crack of dawn on Friday they had acquired put options on your equity, worth $2.2 billion, which they are threatening to sell in the market on Monday, unless you agree to be taken over by them."

Stewart: "You can tell them that we took out put options on them and we bought lots of credit derivatives, and we can take their system down. I can also tell you that we have prepared a scorched-earth defence. We did three trades on our 4.9% stake in BKB with three big investment banks, and we then bought credit-default swaps. Basically we've made sure that the street is full of BKB's name." George has the feeling Stewart has just made this up.

An early story in the *Financial Times*'s Asian edition reports:

> FSB *may not hold enough capital to continue business on Monday if its rumoured obligation to* MBC *still stands, say sources close to British regulators. A letter of comfort in the hands of American banks renders* FSB *liable for* MBC*'s obligations, American bank lawyers say.*

Day 4, Monday August 17th 1998

0700 FSB calls a press conference: "Nothing has happened over the weekend," says McTaggart. "We have $90m exposure to MBC and know nothing of a takeover by German banks. I have never been approached. We have the full support of the British clearers although we never asked for it." Nevertheless, the London Stock Exchange suspends trading in FSB shares, pending clarification.

0745 MBC tells its regulators: "We have no ability to fund ourselves, and as directors we must exercise the option to go into liquidation immediately." Birkenhead calls a press conference and says his bank is "technically insolvent if the obligations under the guarantee are enforced. The regulators have behaved very badly. We are at the wire."

The British banks reviewing their interbank exposure to MBC discover that collectively it is far higher than they thought, around $2 billion each. Was this an unfair blow dealt by the regulators?

0800 De Gier at SBC Warburg: "We are surprised to learn of our new exposure. We say we don't care, we are content to close MBC down. But, as SBC, we may consider our position and pull some major banking operations back to Zurich and Basel."

George calls for calm

0930 The governor of the Bank of England picks this moment, amid rumours that there are queues outside FSB's retail branches, to appear on breakfast TV. FSB is not insolvent, George says, so depositors run a very low risk. Deposits up to £20,000 are anyway guaranteed 90%, and the British Treasury will stand behind the bank if necessary. He denies there is any agreement to sell FSB.

The US Federal Reserve decides to raise interest rates by 0.25%, "because of economic factors, not concerns about systemic risk".

But the D-mark reacts sharply, falling from DM1.75 to DM1.95 to the dollar. "American banks have massively moved the German currency," writes Bloomberg. "American banks are believed to be very unhappy about the reaction of the German authorities to the troubles at BKB."

> *Press Association: The Princes Street branch of FSB in Edinburgh closes its doors after running out of cash. Old ladies and unemployed are queuing three deep on the pavement.*

1110 The British banks suspend FSB from Chaps. They insist on a public announcement of support from Alistair Darling, chief secretary to the Treasury, before reinstating FSB.

1130 Darling calls a press conference. He announces that MBC will go into administration, and that FSB does not face insolvency because the Treasury will stand behind it if necessary: "Widows and orphans can sleep easily in their beds."

1200 The American Treasury and Bank of America discuss the trading out of Elmas's property options, with the Treasury guaranteeing losses. The American banks feel their regulators should have used more leverage.

Newman: "After 30 years of telling everyone to get in line our regulators have just been sort of following."

Fisher: "What they should have said is 'right, you guys are going to support this or we'll consider your banking operations in America'."

1515 The Bundesbank raises interest rates by 0.25%.

The game ends

No one expected the game to reach a conclusion, since it was run against the clock. The objective was to see how far the crisis went in three and a half days. Many more things happened than could be squeezed into these pages. Moreover, many nuances will have been missed – no one participant had the full picture, or a monopoly on the truth.

List of players

Mulhouse Brand & Co (MBC)
Lord Birkenhead, chairman
Peter Butter, chief financial officer
Wendy Nelson, in-house lawyer

Elmas (Emerging Latin Markets Assets and Securities)
Alberto Schultz, president and CEO

Federated Scottish Banks (FSB)
Sir Roy McTaggart, chairman and CEO
Iain Stewart, treasurer
Douglas Firth, lawyer

Bayerische Kreditbank (BKB)
Eugen Toplitz, chairman of the executive board
Hannes Ross, treasurer
Michaela Funk, MBC liaison and lawyer

British officials
Alistair Darling, chief secretary to the Treasury
Howard Davies, chairman, Securities and Investments Board
Eddie George, governor, Bank of England

German officials
Wolfgang Artopoeus, president, BKB Berlin
Jürgen Stark, state secretary, federal finance ministry
Hans Tietmeyer, president, Bundesbank

American officials
Alan Greenspan, chairman, US Federal Reserve
Jim Herzog, acting head, Commodities and Futures Trading Commission
Arthur Levitt, chairman, Securities and Exchange Commission
Robert Rubin, treasury secretary

Multilateral officials
Michel Camdessus, managing director, IMF
Andrew Crockett, general manager, Bank for International Settlements
Wim Duisenberg, president, European Central Bank

British banks

Martin Taylor, chief executive, Barclays Bank
Hans de Gier, chief executive, SBC Warburg
Sir William Purves, chairman, HSBC

German banks

Rolf Breuer, speaker, Deutsche Bank
Jürgen Sarrazin, chairman, Dresdner Bank
Friedel Neuber, chairman, Westdeutsche Landesbank

American banks

Nancy Coburn, chairman, Bank of America
Frank Newman, chairman, Bankers Trust
Dick Fisher, chairman, Morgan Stanley

17 The Sigma affair

Six months into European monetary union there is a crisis, but it has little to do with the euro. It is a classic banking fiasco caused by too many people believing in one man's big idea.

Tuesday July 20th 1999

Perseus Marconi, executive chairman of Sigma Banking Group, a €20 billion conglomerate based in Amsterdam, rides a limo from his canal-side residence to the bank's space-age headquarters in Foppingadreef. He is delighted with his London-based investment bank's huge underwriting of a €5 billion equity issue for Hermes, a phone and satellite company based in Britain, not to mention an additional issue of €3 billion in high-yield bonds. For Marconi, this is the future, the fusion of banking and telecommunications into a single sector – finance and information delivered instantly to any point on the globe – and beyond.

Things have been looking better by the day. A thriving Europe has slowly been pulling world markets out of recession. Stockmarkets have made up a lot of the ground they lost in the second half of 1998. Even bank stocks are improving.

Marconi riffles through his *Financial Times*, hardly glancing at a news item buried at the foot of the front page: "Mobile phone scare widens". But at Sigma's offices the dealing room has already been in uproar for two hours. The American market last night and the Asian markets this morning took the phone scare seriously, dumping any stocks that had been buoyed by mobile phone hardware or franchises and, incidentally, satellite communications too. Why?

Mobile phone scare

Writing in the *New England Journal of Medicine*, scientists at Harvard Business School say new studies leave little or no doubt that mobile phones cause brain tumours. Moreover, a Slovak firm says it has developed a way of encoding short-wave transmissions into long-wave, allowing them to bounce off the ionosphere, making communications satellites redundant. The sharp end of the telecoms industry is suddenly blunted, at least as far as short-termist stock analysts are concerned. The €8 billion equity and debt issue for Hermes has become unplaceable and is stuck on the books of Sigma and its subsidiary MHB Investment

Bank. The bid price for the shares is down to €4.50, less than half the issue price. But that is not the end of the problem. The market suspects the investment bank has not placed the shares, or the debt. The Sigma group also, just yesterday, made a firm bid of $2.1 billion for a mobile phone franchise in China. In America there are fears that Sigma's insurance arm will face heavy claims from mobile phone users with brain tumours. Seeing the entire Sigma group as a telecoms risk as much as a banking risk, banks have started to cancel interbank lending to two Sigma subsidiaries: Great Northern Bank in Britain and Rhein-Ruhr Bank in Germany. Great Northern faces an immediate funding shortfall of £3 billion, which it has to meet by 1700 GMT.

There is another concern. Sigma has been under attack by an American corporate raider, Mega Corp, a media giant, assisted by Wood Stanley, an investment bank. Two weeks ago Mega made a private offer of €15 billion for the group. Marconi refused to talk to Bob Richter, Mega's chairman, because of a long-standing personal feud. The markets are playing into the hands of Mega and Wood Stanley. The raiders do not need to talk down Sigma's share price: it is happening before their eyes. Their plan is to take the group over, strip out the telecoms business, and divide up the banking units for assimilation or sale.

A strangely familiar world

This is the start of what later became known as "The Sigma Affair", a deliberate attempt to bring down one of the world's biggest banks. It is not exactly a conspiracy, but it turns out to be a severe test of the financial system and the people who run it: the regulators, major financial institutions and central bankers.

The banks are fictitious but strangely familiar. Old favourites Chemical Bank and Continental Bank are resurrected. Midshires and Anglia, Bayerische Kreditbank, IBN Flanders Bank and Crédit Général represent the big players of the world financial system. In the eye of the storm is Sigma Bank, which is Dutch regulated, although its major operations are in Britain (MHB and Great Northern Bank) and Germany (Rhein-Ruhr Bank). Apart from its expertise in telecoms finance, Sigma is one of the market leaders in credit derivatives. It has licensed its credit-risk management system, StreetCred40, to 120 other banks.

At Sigma in Amsterdam, Marconi's faith in the integration of telecoms and banking is unshaken, but in the engine room of the bank reality is dawning.

Rufus Franklin, Sigma's chief risk officer – famous for being brilliant but erratic – is faced with a large loss on the Hermes shares that Sigma has underwritten, perhaps up to €8 billion, but the cash is not payable for ten days. His colleagues consider illegally placing some of the shares into investment funds managed by MHB Asset Management, another Sigma subsidiary, which manages $200 billion of assets. But Franklin's more immediate problem is the falling value of Sigma's own portfolio of investments in the shares and bonds of other telecoms companies; these investments have been used as collateral to finance other risk positions in shares and derivatives. The collateral must be topped up as it falls in value, but with what? Franklin hires Fisher King, an American investment bank, to negotiate a block sale of Sigma's equity portfolio, worth €5 billion yesterday but losing value fast.

Europe's central bankers are already concerned about the funding problems at Great Northern Bank and Rhein-Ruhr. They also suspect that Sigma has kept most of the issue of Hermes shares on its own books, having failed to place many shares in the market. The central bankers ask the banks in Britain and the Netherlands to maintain interbank lending at normal levels, to avoid panic.

The international banks consider their positions. Few are heavily exposed to Sigma. They are more concerned with their equity and credit risks in the telecoms sector. But Bayerische Kreditbank (BKB) decides to break ranks and cut off its loans to Rhein-Ruhr Bank, apart from a two-week deposit of €250m that it cannot cancel. The vultures are circling. Britain's Midshires Bank is interested in acquiring Rhein-Ruhr Bank. The maverick Sir Miles Lewis, head of Anglia Bank and once described as "the most dangerous man in the world", loses no time turning others' distress to his advantage. He consults Wood Stanley on how Sigma will be carved up, and expresses interest in some of its investment banking activities.

Tony La Salle, head of corporate finance at Wood Stanley, advises the international banks to "foreclose on Sigma, split up the business and auction it off". The big American banks are slower to see opportunities in the break-up of Sigma.

Sigma defiant

However, Sigma is far from being dead and buried. Marconi will not go down without a fight. Looking suave in his white linen jacket, the man who was once the darling of the London stockmarket reassures the world at an impromptu press conference that Sigma is still wholly committed to the telecoms industry and is unshaken by the market turmoil.

Franklin admits that Sigma holds "pretty much the whole" of the Hermes issue. "But we've always said we would be happy to own the business."

European regulators are slow to co-ordinate their efforts as the crisis builds. During a hastily organised conference call, Jürgen Stark of the German finance ministry takes the initiative: "As government officials we have no formalised system of collaboration," he says, but he proposes that they should collaborate, without making the fact public.

In the European markets, western telecoms stocks have fallen another 20%, and a similar fall is expected in New York when it opens; the Bank of England cuts interest rates by 0.25%

Eddie George, governor of the Bank of England, is reported as saying that Sigma is "solvent and a going concern". Central banks and treasuries are pooling information and ready to provide solvent banks with liquidity. They are adamant this would not include bailing out Sigma. American officials read the situation differently. Robert Rubin, treasury secretary, and Alan Greenspan, chairman of the Federal Reserve, are miffed that the Europeans have not consulted them, but they see a way to get their own back. "Eddie's done two things here," Rubin tells Greenspan. "One, he's going to do a bail-out. Two, this gets us off the hook. We were told by British authorities that Sigma was fine. That allows us to completely isolate this. I'd really hammer Eddie on this one. You tell him 'I'm not supporting that statement unless you're taking full responsibility'."

But Greenspan has one eye on the American economy and possible overheating. Wrong-footing the punters, he raises American interest rates by 0.25%.

Dutch courage

Tom de Swaan, governor of the Dutch central bank, is elected chairman of the consolidated board of European central banks and George, who is not on the governing council of the European Central Bank (ECB), is invited to join. The central bankers decide to order Sigma to offload some of its positions. "The long-term plan," says De Swaan, "if Sigma is insolvent, is that we regulators go in and force the break-up."

Eugen Toplitz, chairman of BKB, continues to give dire warnings of a crash in bonds as well as equities. "The British banks are in a dangerous position," he says. He also worries about how the German banking sector will cope when, as he predicts, "Rhein-Ruhr Bank goes down".

In the Netherlands, the Dutch banks are anticipating the collapse of their biggest rival. It is a bittersweet experience. They do not want to be tarred with the same brush, but "if Sigma goes down," says Jan Chambers, chief risk officer of IBN Flanders Bank, "there will be pickings for us". Gerritt Aesop, the bank's chairman, explains: "We're not interested in buying Sigma, but we are interested in buying assets." He is flabbergasted, however, at the apparent incompetence of his counterpart at Sigma: "Everybody seems to say that the senior management of Sigma is foolish. How come someone who seems to have a reputation for excess is head of a very large bank?" (It has happened before and it can happen again.)

Let the market decide

Chambers predicts that the Sigma crisis "could result in taking 1% off the GDP of Europe". But, he cautions, "the regulators should only intervene if they think there's a serious systemic risk. At this moment it's still concentrated in Sigma Bank. If it stays that way, the market can solve the problem."

Rescuing Sigma would be a mistake, says Aesop. "It would be the Japanese/French type of initiative."

The crisis is not big enough to goad central bankers into a rescue. But they are concerned about the liquidity of Sigma's two commercial and retail banking subsidiaries, Great Northern and Rhein-Ruhr. European officials worry that "informal arrangements between central banks and their banks" may not be enough to avoid a liquidity crisis. Wim Duisenberg, president of the ECB, says: "We want some form of agreement that short-term lines can't be withdrawn."

George is reluctant to pump £3 billion of liquidity, which is more than its own capital, into Great Northern Bank. He tells Howard Davies, chairman of Britain's Financial Services Authority: "I'm not a regulator any more. But I refuse to provide liquidity so you must shut Sigma down."

In theory, none of the euro-zone regulators or central banks is allowed to bail out a bank any more. European monetary union relies on the principle that no single country, or bank, will be bailed out. The ECB is not a lender of last resort. Although Britain is not a member of the euro, the ECB has a legitimate interest in the liquidity of banks in London, which is a big centre for trading in euros and euro-denominated assets. But there is no obvious deus ex machina to support Sigma unless the European banks club together to prop it up. And there is no sign of that – they want to tear Sigma apart.

Meanwhile, Franklin is coming to terms with Sigma's pressing obligations. Although the Hermes proceeds are not payable for ten days, if the shares cannot be sold, Sigma has to raise the cash, perhaps with an enforced sale of assets or subsidiaries. Franklin tells his adviser, Brad Cohen of Fisher King, that the best candidates to buy Great Northern are the British banks Midshires and Anglia, since they have loan exposure to Sigma of $2.5 billion and $3.4 billion respectively, which they might be persuaded to convert to equity. Franklin is also toying with the possibility of temporarily parking offshore some of Sigma's credit portfolio, perhaps by means of a three-month credit-default option, to bring down the bank's regulatory capital requirement.

But European regulators are not impressed by Sigma's attempts to dress up its balance sheet. Stark and other European regulators interrogate Marconi, who admits he is not "a numbers man". Stark tells him: "We're very close to losing all confidence in you as the manager of the Sigma group. We may replace you."

They decide to put Sigma into administration, but it is some time before an administrator is found. In the meantime, Sigma's value is slipping away, with no access to interbank funding, a run on retail deposits, a falling share price and the need to meet margin calls and demands for payments on its credit derivative positions.

Greenspan's edict

Greenspan, mistrusting any figures conveyed to him about the Sigma crisis, attempts to ring-fence his own banking system. In an unprecedented move he forbids American banks to buy any Sigma assets. The banks are flabbergasted.

"Can Greenspan request that?" asks Cohen. Fisher King is not regulated by the Fed, but this seriously undermines its efforts to sell off assets on behalf of Sigma. Mega Corp is not Fed regulated either, so it feels free to pursue its campaign to destroy and then devour Sigma. Wood Stanley's La Salle, acting for Mega, asks Chemical Bank to provide bridging finance. But Rick Strange, Chemical's chairman, heeding threats from Greenspan, is cautiously negative.

Duisenberg and the European regulators tell the press that they have put in place "arrangements to ensure adequate liquidity is available to members of the Sigma group, to avoid discontinuity in their business activities". He explains they will be reviewing appropriate longer-term action. Meanwhile, Marconi and his management team are still in place. But the markets continue to fall.

At the end of the first day of crisis, the financial markets continue to function more or less normally, although billions of dollars have been wiped off stock values. Banks can still generate meaningful value-at-risk figures and assess their credit-risk and market-risk exposures, although correlations between markets are slipping.

Marconi is seen at a new production of *The Damnation of Faust* at Covent Garden with Jack Faraday, Hermes' chairman.

Wednesday July 21st 1999

At Sigma headquarters, the coffee cups and detritus of all-night dealing litter the offices. It has been a tough few hours for Franklin and his senior traders, telephoning banks and investors in Asia to find someone willing to deposit funds. Marconi, well rested after his evening's entertainment in London, lands at Schiphol airport and tells the local press: "We managed to get overnight support from central banks and we're still in one piece."

When he gets to the office he discovers that Franklin has a different view: "We're going to die fairly shortly," Franklin says. Sigma is technically insolvent. "Stocks have fallen 30% overnight so our collateral won't be enough. The central banks accepted the $4 billion portfolio at 50% as collateral. However, my view is that we're bust actually but not publicly. So we should merge with Wood Stanley and Mega Corp immediately."

Marconi will not allow the destruction of his core company: "I'd like to consider selling off subsidiaries before merging."

Anglia Bank's Lewis has a meeting with Franklin, who he judges is more amenable to a sale. He offers to buy 51% of Great Northern Bank, Sigma's British subsidiary, for £1.5 billion, and to take responsibility for £3 billion of its short-term debts.

Bargains in the basement

Franklin ponders the deal: "It was worth £5 billion and we're selling it for £1.5 billion which isn't a catastrophe." But the bigger picture is alarming. "We still have an €8 billion hole in the balance sheet. We've just sold our biggest asset, 25% of the group, for £1.5 billion. That values the group at much less than €8 billion. So this rolling programme of asset disposal is not going to work. And we still have our commitment to pay $2.1 billion for a mobile telecoms franchise in China." The one remaining jewel is MHB Asset Management, which handles clients' funds totalling $200 billion. It should fetch a good price, but not in a distress sale.

There is also the problem of credit derivatives. Sigma is a market leader in credit derivatives. It has its own credit-risk evaluation model, StreetCred40, which is subscribed to by 120 banks. It uses StreetCred40 to price its own portfolio and to make bid-offer prices to its clients, and to some extent to the market at large. This is fine in normal markets. But Sigma's own credit rating has deteriorated and its clients are not prepared to take a risk on its performance, especially on large credit derivatives positions. Sigma's credit derivatives book, with over $100 billion in notional principal, is becoming a millstone round its neck.

IBN Flanders Bank is happy to consider taking over Sigma's matched credit derivatives book. It would act as intermediary on each deal, providing a better credit to the counterparty than Sigma could, and charging a fee that would come out of any proceeds from unwinding the derivatives book. IBN Flanders is also eyeing Rhein-Ruhr Bank, Sigma's subsidiary in Germany, as a means of expanding its operations there.

Chemical Bank is considering converting Sigma debt obligations into equity as a way of getting "some upside potential". Strange asks his regulator Greenspan, in view of his recent embargo on American banks buying bits of Sigma, if there are now "any restrictions on us buying any parts of Sigma, because we're potentially interested in the investment banking operations – MHB Capital, MHB Investment Bank, MHB Securities". Greenspan raises no objection at this stage.

At midday on the second day of the crisis, international banks are seeing the implications of the global telecoms sell-off and its impact on credit spreads and equity prices, deepened by the fear that central banks are far from orchestrating a bail-out. Nor will the American regulators involve themselves in what they see as a European affair. This is a time of recrimination, not constructive effort.

Stand-offish Germans

The German banks are distancing themselves. They are angry about being drawn into a non-German crisis. Toplitz says: "This has begun in the Netherlands. Perhaps it's a European crisis but not especially a German one. So we as German banks don't see why we have to pay the bills."

Greenspan explains why he blocked a merger between Mega Corp and Sigma: "We're not impressed that our friends in Europe have a complete handle on the situation. We think that this whole euro adventure has taken off with a number of teething problems and that some of the regulatory aspects were not fully anticipated."

Rubin adds his own analysis: "Were it not for the Europeans and their sloppy thinking, this mess wouldn't have arisen in the first place."

In a move calculated to irritate the Europeans further, the US Federal Reserve once again raises rates by 0.25% to "head off possible inflationary tendencies in the American economy".

The ECB cuts short-term euro interest rates by 0.25% and may cut them again within the next hour, market sources say. But it seems the American and European regulators are still at odds, with America raising rates and Europe cutting them. Duisenberg gets Greenspan and Rubin on a video link to discuss interest rates and the co-ordination of insurance regulators. Sigma insurance operations in America could draw the country into the crisis.

Rubin notes that insurance regulation on both sides of the Atlantic is somewhat fragmented: "Increasing dependence between banking and insurance raises the question of who would actually jump in at the same time on the insurance side." But he is more preoccupied with the dollar: "We're going up, to try to defend the dollar a little bit. We're up half a point. I don't think we want to go very much further, we're in danger of overcorrecting. But we're not averse to further rises if necessary."

The American Treasury, on behalf of the federal and state insurance commissions, suspends Sigma's insurance subsidiaries from writing further business or paying out commercial claims for a period of five days.

Press reports in London put Sigma's marked-to-market derivatives losses, apart from its matched book, at "at least $5 billion and perhaps as much as $7 billion".

A buying opportunity

Tony Ringo, chief financial officer at Continental Bank, confides to American regulators: "The way we read it, we are the big pockets in town. We've got $50 billion in capital. Chemical has $2 billion exposure to Sigma, we have $800m. We think there's an opportunity to convert it into equity in Sigma. It's an opportunity to take a position in Europe in the telecoms sector."

But a foreign-exchange problem may soon engulf them all. In a memo to Sigma Amsterdam, Sigma New York says: "We're still waiting for the $300m from Ravi Asian Bank through the Chips system. If it doesn't appear we may indeed have liquidity problems." There are reports from East Asia that Ravi Asian "may not open for business tomorrow".

European officials now fear a systemic crisis. They consider putting in clearing functions for foreign-exchange deals in the major currencies, acting as a provider of liquidity for held-up trades. They also consider a worst case if Sigma goes bust. The ideas fly around. They have obviously not done enough collective contingency planning as members of the European System of Central Banks.

Hasty calls by central banks establish that the major banks have foreign-exchange receivables from Ravi Asian Bank totalling $16.2 billion, and that IBN Flanders and Crédit Général are the most heavily exposed ($3.3 billion and $3 billion respectively).

At a Sigma press conference Marconi is jeered and hissed as he takes the rostrum to make what must be his resignation speech. Next to him stands the administrator, Humphrey Bland of Deloitte & Touche. Marconi admits: "I have been destroyed by numbers. I shall go off and start other business ... you will hear from me again."

Stockmarkets are in free fall, with telecoms and banking stocks leading in western as well as emerging markets; there is no safe haven except the Swiss franc and gold

At the end of day two, Sigma is no longer a going concern, although an administrator has been appointed. The foreign-exchange markets are in turmoil, but central banks appear to be stepping into the breach with liquidity where it is needed. The hyenas are tearing up Sigma. A fierce debate rages over credit derivatives and the models used to price them.

Thursday July 22nd 1999

It is the middle of day three. Sigma is contained; central banks have intervened heavily and are prepared to intervene some more; foreign-exchange markets are functioning in slow motion; equity markets are being supported by new credit lines from banks, pre-empting the need for over-extended investors to raise cash from parts of the market that are still liquid. But the situation is precarious. The banking system has been tempted to extend credit to the equity markets way beyond normal banking prudence. If equity markets do not bounce back, who will pick up the pieces?

Bitter conclusion

Can you put the toothpaste back in the tube? After the market mayhem and the collapse of Sigma, the losses of the past 48 hours cannot be reversed. A bubble has burst, and the management of a major bank has been removed. Marconi, visionary though he is, will not get his old job back, and Sigma is dead or dying.

For bankers and regulators, the Sigma affair is a reminder that markets generally grab information and trade on it before examining whether it is good or bad. In this case, governments and financial regulators were quick – perhaps too quick – to intervene to limit the consequences of imprudent banking. Sigma had hardly experienced its first funding problems and been hit by adverse market rumours before the regulators and central bankers were all over it, pumping in liquidity and encouraging its dismemberment and sale.

This is probably symptomatic of the banking landscape in the late 1990s, in which every institution and its components were a target for acquisition or merger. This was good for pre-empting systemic crises, but bad for building businesses and corporate identity.

Sigma went down, but its retail subsidiaries did not. Nor did the financial system, despite a foreign-exchange crisis, a stockmarket crash, and a surprising spat between American and European regulators as the European System of Central Banks learned to flex its muscles. With extraordinary generosity, European central banks subsidised banks to buy shares and stabilise the stockmarkets.

Would governments in real life have pumped in so much cash? Probably. Does that encourage banks – and investors – to take foolish risks? Draw your own conclusions.

The events and dialogue above were compiled from tape-recordings, press releases and notes made by the players. This material is entirely fictitious and in no way represents the behaviour of real-world bankers or government officials, despite the use of some real names.

List of players
Sigma Banking Corporation
Perseus Marconi, chairman and CEO
Rufus Franklin, chief risk officer
Wendy Nelson, in-house lawyer

Rhein-Ruhr Bank
Rainer Eggers, executive chairman

Great Northern Bank
Sir Roy McTaggart, chairman

British banks
Anglia Bank
Sir Miles Lewis, chairman
Rupa Fanshaw, chief financial officer

Midshires Bank
Sir John Furniss, chairman
Harry Duggan, chief risk officer

Other European banks
Bayerische Kreditbank
Eugen Toplitz, executive chairman
Chuck Rivers, chief risk officer

Crédit Général
Charles Lemaitre, chairman
Yvonne Laffitte, chief financial officer

IBN Flanders Bank
Gerritt Aesop, chairman
Jan Chambers, chief risk officer

American banks
Chemical Bank
Rick Strange, chairman
Lynn Darke, chief financial officer

Continental Bank
Bill Speke, chairman
Tony Ringo, chief financial officer

Fischer King
John Friend, chairman
Brad Cohen, chief financial officer

Wood Stanley
Dick Fletcher, chairman
Tony La Salle, head of corporate finance

American officials
Alan Greenspan, chairman, US Federal Reserve
Arthur Levitt, chairman, Securities and Exchange Commission
Robert Rubin, treasury secretary

British officials
Alistair Darling, chief secretary to Treasury
Howard Davies, chairman, Financial Services Authority
Eddie George, governor, Bank of England

German officials
Wolfgang Artopoeus, president, Bayerische Kreditbank
Jürgen Stark, state secretary, federal finance ministry
Hans Tietmeyer, president, Bundesbank

Other European officials
Jean-Claude Trichet, governor, Banque de France
Tom de Swaan, director, Nederlandse Bank

Multilateral officials
Michel Camdessus, managing director, IMF
Andrew Crockett, general manager, Bank for International Settlements
Wim Duisenberg, president, European Central Bank

Others
Karl Bellwether, High Hedge Capital
Hugo Chew, chairman, Ravi Asian Bank
Bob Richter, chairman, Mega Corp

References

Chapter 2

1 Bass, T., *The Eudaemonic Pie*, Houghton Mifflin, 1985; Vintage, 1986; Penguin 1991.

2 Soros, G., *The Alchemy of Finance: Reading the Mind of the Market*, Wiley, 1994.

3 Schwager, J., *Market Wizards*, HarperBusiness, 1994.

Chapter 7

4 Shepheard-Walwyn, T. and Litterman, R., *Building a coherent risk measurement and capital optimisation model for financial firms*, SBC and Goldman Sachs, 1998.

Chapter 8

5 Kupiec, P. and O'Brien, J., *The pre-commitment approach: using incentives to set market risk capital requirements*, The Federal Reserve Board, Finance and Economics Discussion Series, 14, 1997.

6 Calomiris, C.W., *The postmodern bank safety net*, American Enterprise Institute, Washington, DC, 1997.

7 Ely, B., "The cross-guarantee concept: eliminating risk in the interbank markets", *Proceedings*, Federal Reserve Bank of Chicago, May 1999.

Chapter 9

8 Rohner, M. and Shepheard-Walwyn, T., *Equity at Risk: an alternative approach to setting regulatory capital standards for internationally active firms*, IFCI Risk Institute, 2000.

Chapter 12

9 Lascelles, D. and Shirreff, D., *The Fall of Mulhouse Brand*, Centre for the Study of Financial Innovation, London, December 1997.

Chapter 15

10 Michael Lewis is a former Salomon Brothers bond trader and author of *Liar's Poker* (Penguin USA, 1990). He visited his former

colleagues at LTCM after the crisis and described some of the trades on the firm's books.
11 Matthew, xxvi, 52.
12 Jacobs, B., *Capital Ideas and Market Realities*, Blackwell, 1999, p. 293.

Recommended reading

Bernstein, P.L., *Against the Gods: The Remarkable Story of Risk*, Wiley, 1996.

Dunbar, N., *Inventing Money*, Wiley, 2000.
The story of Long-Term Capital Management and the legendary risk managers behind it

Lowenstein, R., *When Genius Failed*, Fourth Estate, 2001.
An account of the failure of Long-Term Capital Management

Taleb, N.N., *Fooled by Randomness: The Hidden Role of Chance in the Markets and in Life*, Texere, 2001.

Glossary of key terms

Actuary
A valuer of insurance portfolios and insurance risks.

Agency problem
The worry that employees' incentives will tempt them to make decisions for personal gain, even if that increases the risks faced by the firm.

ART
Short for alternative risk transfer, the placing of insurance risk outside the insurance industry, for instance with financial investors.

Asset-backed security
A security whose payout is related to the performance of another financial asset, such as a loan, mortgage or lease.

Backwardation
A phenomenon often observed that short-term commodity prices tend to be higher than longer-dated futures prices. The price of the future rises as it approaches its expiry date.

Basel Committee, Basel 1 and 2
A committee of bank supervisors that meets regularly in Basel, Switzerland, to set guidelines for banks' prudential capital requirements. Basel 1 is a set of its guidelines published in 1988 and still in force. Basel 2, its replacement, scheduled for implementation by 2007, has been under development since about 1998.

Bayesian mathematics
A method of inferring wider patterns and probabilities on the basis of limited data. (Named after Reverend Thomas Bayes, 1702–61.)

Beta
The volatility of a company's share price relative to a market index.

Black-Scholes

A formula for valuing options, particularly stock options, developed by Fischer Black and Myron Scholes in the 1970s.

Brady bond

A bond issued by a developing country to replace rescheduled debt. Named after Nicholas Brady, American treasury secretary from 1988 to 1993. The principal is usually guaranteed by American treasury bonds.

Call option

The right but not the obligation to buy an asset at a previously agreed price within a specified period.

Cap

A form of insurance that pays out if a floating interest rate rises above a specified level.

CAPM

Capital Asset Pricing Model, a theory of market behaviour which holds that prices find their level according to all available information. If all participants have the same information, it is impossible to beat the average return.

CAT bond

Catastrophe bond – a bond whose value or coupon is designed to absorb losses if a specified insured event occurs, usually an earthquake or storm damage. The capital value or interest due is reduced according to losses incurred.

Chinese wall

An information barrier imposed between departments of the same financial or professional firm to guard against the flow of sensitive information and other possible conflicts of interest in serving different clients.

Clearing

The process of checking the creditworthiness of a party to a transaction before allowing the transaction to go through.

Collateral

A pledge of cash, securities or other assets as a guarantee for a financial position on which money is or may be owed.

CDO

Short for collateralised debt obligation, a package of loans, bonds or other credit risks, diversified to produce more stable returns than single named credits. The package is often re-divided into tranches, each tranche being priced and sold according to the expected probability of loss or impaired value.

Concentration risk

Putting all your eggs in one basket; that is, a group of risk exposures that are likely all to be lossmaking under the same circumstances.

Contango

When spot prices become lower than futures prices (see Backwardation).

Correlation

The extent, on a scale of 0 to 1, to which price changes in one market or financial instrument follow the same pattern as price changes in another market or instrument; the opposite of diversification.

Counterparty

The other party to a bilateral transaction.

Covered call or warrant

An option to buy an asset at a specified price, sold by the holder of the asset.

Credit default swap

A contract to pay the full value of an asset if it is affected by a specified credit event, such as a default, on delivery of the impaired asset.

Credit event

An instance of default or insolvency severe enough to trigger a credit default swap.

Credit insurance

Insurance against loss through default or other credit impairment.

Credit risk

The risk that a counterparty will fail to meet its debt obligations in a timely fashion.

Currency swap

An agreement between two parties to exchange cash flows in different currencies.

Default

Failure to pay obligations in a timely fashion.

Derivative

A financial instrument derived from an underlying asset, or from an index representing asset prices.

Discounted debt

A loan or bond, the selling price of which is reduced either because of the borrower's default, or because of its perceived likelihood of default in future.

Dynamic or delta hedging

Monitoring a hedging position and adjusting it according to market movements rather than hedging the entire exposure.

Efficient market theory

The theory that markets in which complete information is uniformly shared will provide no more than an average return (see also CAPM).

Emerging markets

Markets for securities or other financial instruments sold by issuers located outside the ten or so leading industrial countries.

Fair value

The theoretical value of an asset or a portfolio of assets if it had to be sold in the market today.

FAS 133

Financial accounting standards introduced in America in 2001 which stipulate "fair value" accounting for most derivative positions.

Floating rate

An interest rate that is reset at intervals according to a specified benchmark, such as LIBOR (the London interbank offered rate).

Futures

Contracts to deliver a commodity or a financial asset at a certain price at a future date.

Hedge

A financial position that offsets the perceived risks of an asset or liability held by the same entity.

Hedge fund

An investment fund that aims to use sophisticated trading methods, including derivatives, to produce consistent positive returns.

Hypotheticals

Make-believe business or political scenarios, talked through by experts, to explore outcomes or to test emergency procedures.

Illiquid

Difficult to buy or sell because of limited or non-existent supply or demand.

In the money

Describes an option that has positive market value.

Interest-rate swap

A bilateral contract to exchange cash flows based on two different interest-rate scales, for instance one fixed, one floating.

Junk bond

A bond usually issued by a company of risky credit quality, paying a high margin above prevailing interest rates to compensate for a high risk of default.

Lender of last resort

Usually a government or central bank that is expected to support financial institutions at times when they have funding or liquidity problems.

Leverage, leveraged

The ratio of a borrower's debt in relation to its capital base; the higher the ratio of debt to capital, the more leveraged it is.

LIBOR

The London interbank offered rate, an interest rate set daily for various currencies by international banks in London.

Liquid, liquidity

Relatively easy to buy or sell because of ample supply and demand; a measure of the ease of buying and selling.

Margin, margin call

Cash or other assets pledged to offset lossmaking positions with a counterparty or with an exchange; a demand for such cash or assets as the calculated loss increases.

Mark to market

To value an asset, liability or other position according to today's market price (see also Fair value).

Marketmaking

Undertaking to quote continuously buying and selling prices for a particular asset and to deal with market participants at those prices.

Mezzanine

A type of loan financing, riskier than senior debt, often with equity-like characteristics. It pays high interest and may include a share of the company's profits or a right to convert into shares.

Model

A formula or simplified structure that seeks to replicate or explain the behaviour of a market or a financial instrument, usually with the aim of calculating future probable price movements.

Monte Carlo simulation

The iteration by computer of many possible random outcomes – like spinning a roulette wheel many times.

Moral hazard

The risk that reckless action will be encouraged by the presence of a guarantee, or of a perceived lender of last resort.

Net present value

The value today of a financial asset payable or maturing at some time in the future, discounting the cost of borrowing the money to finance it.

NRSRO

Nationally Recognised Statistical Rating Organisation, a rating agency that is officially recognised by the American Securities and Exchange Commission (see rating agency).

Off-balance-sheet credit risk

An estimate of the loss that would be incurred if a counterparty to a bilateral derivative transaction or a contingent liability (which do not appear on the standard balance sheet) became insolvent.

Omega

A measure of the risk/reward characteristics of one or more securities taking into account the investor's performance goals and its agreed tolerance of loss.

On the run

The most heavily traded in a class of debt instruments, for instance benchmark government bond issues or issues of commercial paper by the most creditworthy borrowers.

Operational risk

A financial institution's exposure to the risk of loss resulting from inadequate or failed internal processes, people and systems or from external events.

Opportunity cost

The return likely to be forgone by deciding against, or being prevented from, taking a course of action.

Option
The right, but not the obligation, to buy or sell an asset at a set price at some time in the future.

Out of the money
Describes an option that has negative market value.

Over-the-counter
A bilateral transaction rather than one dealt on a multilateral exchange.

Particle finance
A separation of financial risks into their smallest tradable components.

Poisson distribution
Developed by Siméon-Denis Poisson (1781–1840), a formula to determine probability given a small number of observed events.

Portfolio
A set of assets held as an investment.

Pre-commitment
A proposal that the amount of banks' regulatory capital should be set and adjusted according to the banks' own forecasts of their likely unexpected losses.

Quanto swap
A swap, usually a currency swap, in which the cash flows in one currency are indexed to the floating interest rate, or exchange rate, of a different currency.

Raroc
Risk-adjusted return on capital, a concept developed to measure the profitability of a financial institution, or one of its divisions, in terms of the amount of capital it has put at risk.

Rating agency
Evaluates the creditworthiness of issuers of debt securities – it grades bond issues according to the likelihood of the borrower not paying up.

Secondary market

The buying and selling of securities or other financial assets once they have been introduced to the market.

Securities

Tradable certificates, usually bonds or shares, which promise either future payments or a share of future proceeds.

Settlement, settlement risk

Proven transfer of an item of value, such as a security or a payment, from the account of the seller to the account of the buyer; the risk that such a settlement will not be completed.

Sharpe ratio

A value that measures the performance of an investment portfolio against its tendency to fluctuate in value. The higher the ratio, the better, in theory, is the risk-adjusted performance. (Named after William Sharpe, Nobel prizewinner, 1990.)

Sovereign debt

Debt issued or guaranteed by a sovereign country.

Spread

The difference between the price at which a security or other asset is traded and a comparable benchmark rate; or the difference between the buying price and the selling price.

Subordinated debt

Debt issued by a borrower which ranks below senior debt but above equity. In the case of a liquidation, the senior debt gets paid first, then the subordinated debt.

Stress-testing

Calculating the effect of extreme events on financial instruments, or on the health and wealth of financial institutions, even of the world financial system.

Strike price

The agreed price at which an option may be exercised.

Swap

An agreement to exchange cash flows based on fixed or variable rates, or on any specified index.

Swaption

An option to enter a swap agreement at a set rate at some time in the future.

Syndicated loan

A loan arranged by one bank or a small group of banks, then often parcelled out to many other banks.

Ultra vires

The Latin for "beyond one's powers", referring in financial dealings to an action by a financial officer that is outside his or her authority.

Unbundling

Dividing a complex financial instrument or a set of risks into its component parts, for the purposes of hedging or partial sale.

Underlying

The financial asset or liability on whose price or behaviour a derivative instrument is based.

VaR

Short for value-at-risk, a calculation of the likely maximum loss, according to recent market volatility, that a financial asset, portfolio of assets, or an entire financial institution, could suffer in the near future.

Volatility

A measure of the intensity of price changes experienced by a security or other financial asset over a specified period.

Warrant

A certificate that empowers the holder to buy a security or other asset at a specified price during a certain period.

INDEX

Numbers in *italics* indicate Figures; those in **bold** indicate Tables.

A

B

G

H

I

U

V

W

Z